MEDITATION
for
INNER PEACE

MEDITATION

for

INNER PEACE

YOUR GUIDE
TO RELAXATION
& TRUE HAPPINESS

EDDIE & DEBBIE SHAPIRO

PIATKUS

© 1997 Eddie and Debbie Shapiro

First published in 1997 by
Judy Piatkus (Publishers) Ltd
5 Windmill Street, London W1P 1HF
www.piatkus.co.uk

Reprinted 1998 (twice), 2000

The moral right of the authors has been asserted

A catalogue record for this book is
available from the British Library

ISBN 0-7499-1417-3

Edited by Esther Jagger
Designed by Sue Ryall
Artwork by Tamara Sternberg

References for artwork on pp. 138-9
supplied by the Prison Phoenix Trust

Set in Goudy by Action Typesetting Ltd, Gloucester
Printed and bound in Great Britain by
Biddles Ltd, www.biddles.co.uk

We dedicate this book to all our teachers both past and present, and to Lex Hixon for the gift of his life. May all beings be free from suffering.

Contents

PART ONE   PATH OF TRANSFORMATION

Chapter 1   Finding Your Way Out of the Maze   3
   Practice – Soft Breath   *12*

Chapter 2   Ascent from the Brain's Basement   14
   Practice – Body Scan   *18*
   Practice – Just Being   *29*

Chapter 3   Turning Muddy Water into Sweet Milk   31
   Practice – Clarifying Priorities   *35*
   Practice – Noting and Labelling   *39*
   Practice – Extending Appreciation   *46*

Chapter 4   The Lotus Blooms in the Sun   49
   Practice – Anytime Metta   *58*
   Practice – Healing Heart Meditation   *65*

PART TWO   RELEASE, RELAX, RENEW

Chapter 5   *Letting It All Go*   69
Practice – Instant Inner Conscious Relaxation   78

Chapter 6   *How ICR Works*   81
Practice – Inner Conscious Relaxation No.1   85
Practice – Inner Conscious Relaxation No.2   90

Chapter 7   *All in the Mind's Eye*   94
Practice – Hot Hands   97
Practice – Trading Places with the Buddha   102
Practice – Journey to Your Inner Truth   105

PART THREE   AWAKENNG THE SLEEPING BUDDHA

Chapter 8   *The Journey Is the Goal*   111
Practice – Just Breathing   115

Chapter 9   *On Being Still*   127
Practice – Posture Perfect   141
Practice – Breathing In, Breathing Out   147

Chapter 10   *Many Paths Up the Mountain*   149
Practice – Breath Awareness Meditation   154
Practice – Witness Meditation   156
Practice – Mantra Meditation   160
Practice – Candle Gazing Meditation   162
Practice – Metta Meditation   164
Practice – Forgiveness Meditation   168
Practice – Walking Meditation   172

Tapes and Workshops   174

Bibliography   176

Index   178

PART ONE

PATH OF
TRANSFORMATION

Chapter 1

Finding Your Way Out of the Maze

We were sitting in a coconut grove, the sun shining through the broad, flat palm leaves. 'Are you happy today?' The monk broke into a wide grin from ear to ear, white teeth glistening in his crinkled, brown face, illuminated by his orange robe. 'Are you happier today than you were yesterday?' Despite his humorous tone his question was a genuine one. A group of us were in retreat and had been practising meditation all that day and all the previous day, and there were eight more days to go. If we were not beginning to feel happier as a result, then what was the purpose of being there? Achaan Maha Dharma Tam was not just asking us if we were happy, he was teaching us that the very purpose of meditation is to find the inner peace that is our deepest happiness.

Every day for ten days he asked us the same question. And each day it drew us deeper into looking at ourselves. It highlighted the extent to which we were holding on to our concerns, doubts and conflicts, how difficulties can actually feel more real and meaningful than joy, how hard it was to trust happiness, even that we had forgotten what happiness meant. It showed us how easy it is to dismiss the importance of happiness and, instead, how we tend to focus more on what is wrong.

The belief that meditation should make us happy is not shared by everyone. In some traditions we hear that meditation is hard work and takes enormous effort; elsewhere we hear that we should have no expectations or hopes of achieving anything from our practice, even that the practice itself is boring.

Yet what our Thai monk was telling us, in his own way, was that there is enough pain and suffering in the world already – the very nature of life includes change and unfulfilled desire and the longing for things to be different from how they are, all of which brings discontent and dissatisfaction. He was teaching us that through the practice of meditation we can actually connect with who we are and find a deeper contentment: an acceptance of life as it is, without a clinging to desire or a fear of change, and that this can bring a lasting and pervading inner peace. It was a liberating and uplifting realisation.

Sleeping Buddhas

This level of joy is attainable by each one of us, for the very essence of every person is basically good, basically free. We are all Buddhas, even if we are still sleeping Buddhas who have yet to awaken. The potential for happiness is equally present in everyone, yet we lose touch with that potential, lose touch with our innate peace, and come to believe that it is somewhere beyond our reach. We are used to life being stressful or difficult – it is familiar – whereas happiness is unfamiliar. We consider it to be self-indulgent, or do not trust it to last. Psychologist Robert Holden, who founded the first NHS Laughter Clinic and leads workshops on finding happiness, says we normally think of happiness as something we have to deserve, earn, work for or pay for. We do not believe that we could be happy at any time, even without a reason, let alone that happiness is our birthright.

Instead we find ourselves in a maze, going round in circles, trying to find a way out, trying to break the cycles of habitual patterns and behaviour. How many times have you wanted to change your daily routine that leaves so little space for quiet or solitary time, yet you feel trapped by commitments? Or do you long to spend more time relaxing or meditating, but feel guilty because you think you should be caring for others instead? Do you know you are trying to do too much but find it difficult to ask for help? Pressures seem to come from every direction and all you want to do is stand up and scream – but you don't. You know you are getting stressed, or at the least that you are not at peace; you keep trying to find some level of release through work or family or entertainment, while simultaneously not trusting the happiness you do find.

Yet, inside, you know that this is not all there is to it. You look at your children, see their laughing, playful freedom, and know you were once like that; or you look at spiritual leaders such as the Dalai Lama and a part of you resonates, as if in recognition, at the serenity of such beings. Somewhere inside each one of us we know we have the potential for far greater happiness, that such joy and peace are within us too. But what will it take to find that happiness? How do we awaken our sleeping Buddha?

'To be truly happy is a revolutionary act,' writes Sharon Salzberg in *Loving Kindness*, 'because it depends upon a revolution within ourselves.' Is it time now for your revolution, for a turning around of yourself in response to your life, your relationships, your purpose of being?

Internalising the External

If you answered yes to the above question then your challenge is to connect with the inner peace and unconditional happiness that is your birthright. In so doing you will be seeking a balance between your outer activities – whether work, play, sports or family time – and your inner world, through deep relaxation, visualisation, prayer or meditation. It is a big challenge, for each of us has to do it for ourselves – we cannot buy serenity or joy in a bottle, or get it from a therapist's couch. Peace is already inside us, and the real challenge is to realise this.

The way to achieve it is to take time to withdraw your participation, to internalise your energy instead of externalising it, to tap into the beauty within. 'To go out of your mind at least once a day is tremendously important,' writes Alan Watts in *Meditation*. 'By going out of your mind you come to your senses.' Going out of your mind does not mean becoming thoughtless, inane or vague, but is a release from the confines of the habitual, repetitive and neurotic mind. As a result you can enter into a spaciousness and freedom, an inner quiet that awakens the creative, aware and truly sane mind. This brings energy and joy into your being, enriching you on every level.

In other words you start seeing that life is to be *lived*. 'To live is not merely to survive,' writes Matthew Fox in *Original Blessing*. 'Living implies beauty, freedom of choice, giving birth, discipline, celebration. Living is not the same as going shopping or buying, nor is it the same as making a nest in which to escape the sufferings of one another.' The experience of such an alive life is available to each one of us, if we just take the time to let go and be at ease.

The Way In

Deep relaxation is like pressing an erase button to remove the tension, frustration, resistance and confusion of our inner tape recorders. As we sink into a greater ease within ourselves, the more we feel comfortable with who we are and the easier it becomes to function naturally; the more we relax, the more alive we become. In this sense, relaxation is a process of inducing complete and profound physical, mental and emotional rest, putting us back in touch with our original, natural state.

True relaxation can only occur when we systematically relax each part of the brain as well as the body. The method described in this book is called Inner Conscious Relaxation (ICR) and has its origins in the ancient texts of India known as the tantra shastras. In the late 1960s Eddie began to study yoga and became a swami (yogi) in India. He trained with Sri Swami Satchidananda and Paramahansa Satyananda, both highly respected yoga masters. Satyananda personally taught him this ancient art of relaxation known as Yoga Nidra, within the context of self-realisation.

Satyananda believed that true relaxation is the path to self-knowledge. If we are to become free of that which limits us, we need to go deep into the core of our being. Eddie's training in India was both profound and effective. It showed him that the cause of our unease is not so much the traumas themselves, with their attendant pain and discomfort, as the tension caused by the trauma. We spend so much time looking back at events that have happened to us, but we need to put just as much time into releasing the tension held as layers of unconscious stress in the mind and body.

Over the many years during which we have been teaching ICR we have slowly refined the practice to meet the varying needs of busy Western lives, which are so different from those in ancient India. In particular we have realised the need for ICR to be based in the heart as an expression of loving acceptance towards ourselves. Self-esteem and self-acceptance are critical – few people feel at ease with themselves – and such states undermine our whole way of being. The mind is confused and demanding when lost in worries, doubts and fears; it is easily self-obsessed and unable to let go. It is only when we can go beneath that level of the mind that we leave behind such chaos and connect with that which is quiet and peaceful.

Where relaxation is a complete and conscious letting go, meditation focuses the mind into ever deeper states of absorption. The state of meditation is essentially a spontaneous experience that occurs when the sense of ourselves as a separate entity drops away and there is simply an experience of being, empty and free. It may have happened to you at a moment when you were completely absorbed in what you were doing – perhaps walking or sitting quietly on a beach or in a wood, perhaps listening to music, or doing something particularly creative and engrossing. The sense of yourself as isolated or separate is no longer there. In its place is everything else, as if you have merged into the sky, the birds, the trees, the notes being played. It is a state described in Buddhism as both emptiness and form. It is empty as there is no separate 'I' present; yet it is form as it contains all life.

The purpose of practising meditation is to come closer to this awareness, where we can consciously enter a place of profound peace. The breath is the main tool we use, for when we follow the rhythm of the breath it immediately internalises our focus, drawing us in. The breath is also a great teacher, for although it gives us life it is not ours to own – it is ours only when we are willing to release it. Through watching the breath we have the chance to see ourselves clearly as we are and to enter into deeper levels of awareness and insight. Traditional forms of meditation focus on developing either a clear and awake mind or a compassionate and loving heart.

While Eddie was practising yoga in India, Debbie was training in meditation in London. By the time we came together in the mid-1980s we had both had many years of practice, yet still had much to learn from each other. In particular, we have seen how essential it is to be relaxed before we meditate. Perhaps like many people, you want to learn meditation as an aid to stress release, but when you try to focus your mind on being still your physical, psychological or emotional stress immediately surfaces. Sounds familiar? It is much harder to be concentrated or absorbed if you are not relaxed. Instead, you will be reliving the stress, going over the different aspects of it in your mind and looking for solutions, or sitting there feeling uptight and irritated. How can you watch the breath when you are experiencing an endless stream of unresolved scenarios? Very quickly your body will start to ache, your mind will be going overtime and you will be constantly looking at the clock. You will then come to the conclusion that you cannot meditate, you're obviously a lost cause, so what's the point of trying?

If, on the other hand, you take the time to relax first, all these tensions will be eased and you will be able to sink more deeply into the quiet space within. So we highly recommend you to do either a deep relaxation session before meditation, or some simple stretching movements, such as yoga, to loosen the body, followed by a few minutes of deep breathing. If you follow this routine the benefits of meditation will be far greater.

To make this process easier to follow, we have divided the book into three sections. In this first part we explore the psychological and emotional changes that occur as we move from a state of stress and tension to one of inner ease and freedom; in the second part we talk about the process of relaxation – what it is and how to do it; while in the third part we explore the many facets of meditation and offer directions and guidance. Throughout the book there are also practices for you to do to release stress and discover a greater ease.

Simply Being

Inner peace arises naturally as we go beneath the layers of doubt and confusion, fear and anxiety. It does not depend on any external state, person, activity or condition, for true peace and happiness cannot be conditional – it cannot be dependent on anything or anyone for it to occur. As all phenomena are temporary and impermanent, so happiness based on that would be equally insubstantial, leading to disappointment and frustration.

Yet how often do we make our happiness conditional? How often do we base our joy on superficial or temporary things? 'When this happens then I'll be happy ...' or 'I can't be at peace until ...' or 'I'll be fine when I'm in love/older/richer/healthier,' and so on. Take a moment to look at what conditions you are imposing on yourself, in what ways you are limiting your joy. Does it depend on your children or partner being happy? On being recognised at work? On losing weight? On having more money? These things are fine in themselves, but to connect with the source of your peace is a far greater gift. Mary came to one of our workshops and was adamant about wanting to be at peace.

However, she was soon confronted with her belief that she felt she could not be happy until she knew her children and her grandchildren were happy. Is your happiness always somewhere in the future, like a gleaming prize awaiting you when all your suffering is over? Do you keep putting it off?

Or perhaps you are limiting your joy because others find it difficult or threatening to see you at ease when they are not. Does your happiness seem to enhance their misery? Jane, a delightful, lively eighty-two-year-old who came to one of our programmes, lives in an assisted housing complex. But she was being ostracised by the other residents as she never had anything to complain about, she was at ease with her life and loved to practise yoga and to meditate. Her neighbours found this difficult as it highlighted their own conflicts and limitations. We are not talking about a superficial happiness here, one that denies the reality of pain, but a really deep joy of being alive, an appreciation of our existence that embraces both pain and joy while also going deeper.

To what extent have you been conditioned to believe that you do not deserve to be happy, or taught to mistrust happiness? Conditioning can be very powerful, influencing every aspect of our lives, and we rarely question its validity. Did you grow up believing that happiness never lasts, that you have to work or pay for it, or that life is meant to be a struggle? If we believe that we do not have a right to be happy, we must question that belief and look further.

Being at peace in a world full of conflict and struggle does not mean we are denying the pain, but it does mean listening to our own inner truth. By internalising our attention – through relaxation and meditation – we become aware of the depth and beauty of our own selves, of the value and importance of every living creature, every act of nature, every work of art, every moment of life. We enter into a world of meaning and resonance. The happiness that

Achaan Maha Dharma Tam was talking about is a happiness that is always present. There is no need to look anywhere outside of us, but we will find it only when we are still long enough to be present with it.

Just stop and be still is all we need to do. Just be in the stillness, breathing, letting go, being still. It only takes one moment to be still. All the truth is within that stillness; peace is in that stillness. When we are fully present and experience the moment in the moment, then the way out of the maze becomes clear – there are no more questions, there is no need for answers. Just be still. 'Meditation is the discovery that the point of life is always arrived at in the immediate moment,' writes Alan Watts in *Meditation*. 'We find there is only a present, only an eternal now.'

Practice – Soft Breath

The simple act of breathing is our greatest saviour. When pressures are building and demands become overwhelming, the first place that shows signs of stress is the breath. It becomes progressively more shallow and rapid until we are only breathing in the top part of the lungs. When we take a deep breath, filling our lungs all the way down as if into our belly, and then blowing the air out through our mouth, it releases any tension. Through the breath we can become quiet, more centred, more still. We can focus on our breath at any time, anywhere, so that it becomes a true friend.

So begin by practising breath release. Find a comfortable place to sit with your back straight, your shoulders slightly back and your chest relaxed. Take a deep breath in, filling your lungs, and as you blow it out let it take all your tension with it. Breathe out your tension. As you breathe deeply, say to yourself: *soft belly, soft belly, soft belly.* Let your breath fill your belly and soften any tension that is there. Do this a few times.

Then come back to your normal breathing pattern and just watch your breath for a few minutes – just watching as it enters and leaves your body. Then take another deep breath and this time say to yourself: *soft heart, soft heart, soft heart.* Breathe into the area of your heart – the heartspace – and let your breath soften any resistance there may be. Breathe out tension, breathe in softness and ease, mercy and compassion. Do this a few times, then return to your normal breathing.

Watch the breath coming in and out for a few minutes – just observing the flow of your natural breath. This exercise is an important step in discovering a deeper level of innate ease and joy.

Chapter 2

Ascent from the Brain's Basement

When we first met Michael at one of our workshops he epitomised so many people who have to deal with high stress levels and wonder how to make it through each day. A schoolteacher in a run-down area of a big city, Michael taught teenagers history, a subject that most of them were not in the least bit interested in learning. He was suffering from high blood pressure and clinical depression and was ready to leave his job. Daily he found himself unable to control his classes without shouting or verging on violence. Already dosed with medication, before resigning Michael decided to try one other route. He began to practise Inner Conscious Relaxation every day for thirty minutes. After a few months he began to alternate that with Metta, a meditation practice aimed at developing loving kindness and compassion.

A year later we met Michael again. He had changed. No longer on any form of medication, he was not only enjoying teaching but had been promoted to head of department. His high blood pressure had come down, the depression had lifted, and he was able to recognise early warning signs of rising anger and to take the necessary steps to dissipate it before it reached boiling point. He looked at least ten years younger.

Michael is no exception. The stresses and pressures of work, finances, relationships, children and maintaining all the various aspects of life confront each one of us. The demands can seem endless, and unless we take time out to work with ourselves they easily become overwhelming. The result may be physical symptoms such as ulcers, headaches, indigestion, nervous disorders, exhaustion or impotence; or psychological and emotional disorders such as irritability, anger, control or power issues, guilt, shame and fear. This is known as the *stress response*.

But just as Michael is no exception in his manifestation of stress symptoms, nor is he an exception in being able to work with those symptoms and to find a more fulfilling approach to life. We can all do this.

The Distress of Stress

Stress itself is not bad. Despite an enormous amount of media coverage telling us how to manage stress and how to live a stress-free life, the fact is that stress is an integral part of our every waking moment – it is the dynamic flow between two opposing forces that creates a positive reaction, as in a bridge that is dependent on the stress between the various parts in order to stay in place. In the work environment, stress can be the stimulation needed to meet demanding challenges, the force that encourages us to reach greater levels of understanding. There can even be an enjoyment of the sense of elation or self-esteem that accompanies stress, so that we begin to crave or seek out stress-producing situations.

Generally, however, our reaction to stress is an initial high, followed by exhaustion and adverse psychological or physical effects, such as the debilitation of concentration and efficiency. Stress turns to distress when our response to it becomes pressured, fearful or overwhelmed.

'My life had started to fall apart – it was as if all the traumas of my thirty-four years hit me all at once. I had always coped so well, although too busy with my career and family to look at the emptiness of it all. Now a lack of meaning was being shown in regular emotional outbursts at home. My husband and son called these my "tin hat days". As my outbursts became worse my husband would withdraw further from me. I felt empty, trapped, a victim, worthless.'

Julia

'I was absolutely desperate for a peaceful life. I remember saying to myself, "I can't stand being like this any longer."'

Barbara

'I was a nervous, edgy, emotional person – my life was busy and very stressful. I found it difficult to relax, rather I felt driven to achieve and keep on top of things. I needed to be seen to be all right.'

Margaret

Stress is not an external entity that we have to suffer. Whatever the various factors we are dealing with, it is how we respond to these factors that determines our stress level. In other words, if we think we are getting stressed, the more stressed we will become. The same things may happen to two people but their responses may differ, depending on their state of mind, beliefs and attitudes. One may feel quite overwhelmed and unable to cope, and gets angry; the other may calmly deal with the situation and then later take time out to rest and relax. In this way we see that stress is not simply an external factor that is or is not present, but is our response to the situations that confront us. So whether we are an executive facing a room full of board members or a childminder facing a room full of two-year-olds, whether we are experiencing overwork or extreme boredom, relationship problems or loneliness, the stress-producing potential is the same as it is within us, not in the situation.

And the truth is that most of us respond to stress with more stress, for few of us have learnt how to develop a natural state of inner relaxation and ease. According to a number of reports, 70–80 per cent of visits to GPs are stress-related. The British Safety Council reported in 1995 that each year in Britain approximately 90 million working days are lost due to stress-related issues at a cost to businesses of about £5 billion, and that more than 150,000 people in Britain now receive counselling for stress-related issues, twice as many as ten years ago. In America it is even higher – stress problems cost the economy up to $75 billion per year.

As stress becomes distress we begin to live in a world dominated by fear and anxiety. Problems seem insurmountable, we over-react to making simple decisions, we get muddled and unable to think clearly, we rage and lose control over meaningless issues, or our behaviour becomes erratic and unpredictable. Feeling out of control, as if at the hands of some external force that determines our psychological state, we easily lose touch with ourselves and how we think and feel, we get locked into critical mind states that prove we are failures or are undeserving. We forget about giving or sharing, about celebrating and appreciating life. In other words, we stop fully living.

Practice – Body Scan

(15–30 minutes)

The body scan enables us to assess our bodies and the tension being stored in different areas, and then it helps to release that tension. This can be done at home, in a park, or even on a train. Find a quiet place either to sit or to lie down – somewhere you will be undisturbed for at least fifteen minutes. For any longer, do it lying down with a light blanket to cover you. Settle yourself and close your eyes. For a few moments just watch your breath as it enters and leaves your body.

All you are going to do is move your mind through your body, area by area, and simply pay attention to the sensations you find, such as tension or tightness, tingling or heat. Let your breath release and relax.

Now *slowly* begin to scan your body, starting at your toes. Take your mind to your toes ... feet ... ankles ... up your legs to your knees and thighs. Breathe into your legs and feet, and feel them releasing and relaxing with each out breath.

From the legs bring your attention to your buttocks ... lower back ... middle back and upper back. Breathing into your back, becoming aware of any tension and releasing it through your breath.

Now bring your mind to your genitals ... belly ... abdomen, slowly moving upwards to your chest and to your shoulders. Breathing in and releasing.

Now start in your fingers and breathe into your hands ... wrists ... arms ... elbows and back to your shoulders. Breathing and relaxing. Take your time. And then up through your neck to your jaw, breathing and relaxing, through all the areas of your face ... the back of your head and the top of your head.

Now just breathe. Let your breath flow through you like waves on the shore. If you want to you can repeat the body scan, but this time do it a little more quickly, simply assessing any changes in the way your body feels. When you are ready, have a good stretch before you get up.

The Stress Response

The *stress response* is the way in which we react to stress factors. It is seen in our psychological and physical reactions as we confront demanding circumstances that are too much for us to cope with. This sets off the alarm bells. Our state of mind is directly related to our state of health – it is impossible to separate the two. Consequently, as we experience greater pressure from the world around us to perform or act in a certain way, that pressure finds its expression through our physical health.

When a stress factor triggers a response in the brain, the first thing that happens is the sounding of an alarm. That starts a reaction in the limbic system, where our emotional states are first registered and felt. This area also regulates the nervous system, which monitors the heart rate, digestion and metabolism, blood pressure, respiration and reproduction. And yet we wonder why we get stomach ulcers, high blood pressure, palpitations, nervous disorders or sexual problems!

The alarm triggers the release of the hormone adrenalin, needed for a fight-or-flight reaction. This slows down our digestive system in order to save energy, speeds up the heart rate to provide more energy, and generally affects the whole body. As tension accumulates we not only have mood swings, irrational behaviour and emotional outbursts but also suffer from backache, constipation or diarrhoea, grinding teeth, hyperventilation, loss of appetite, excessive sweating, skin rashes or insomnia.

Part of the problem comes from our lifestyle. In the days of primitive man we would have used the rush of adrenalin to enable us to confront and fight or to run and hide – whichever was more necessary for survival. Present-day causes of stress that trigger adrenalin are not so life-threatening: it can be coursing through our bodies in response to a child knocking over a glass of orange juice, followed by receiving a couple of unexpected bills in the post, getting stuck in a traffic jam or being late for a meeting. We may want to scream – which would use some of that flight-or-fight energy – but society does not support such behaviour. With nowhere for the adrenalin to go, it has a slowly debilitating effect on the body. If this scenario continues on a regular basis our reserves are soon depleted and we are on edge, unable to let go, easily upset for no reason. Soon we become physically out of balance, exhausted and unresponsive.

'I was working in a nursing home. Caring for the elderly can be stressful at the best of times, but when it is your job you have little chance to recuperate. Part of the difficulty is the constant demand for assistance, care or attention. It can seem as if it is all one-way – a giving without anything being given. After about six months of this, one evening Eddie and I were having dinner. He asked me to pass the salt. And suddenly I cracked! I raged at him for a few minutes about asking me to do something, although I quickly saw that it was not him I was really raging at. I was raging at myself. I had nothing left to give, yet deep inside I wanted to give unconditionally, to be able to give endlessly, without limitation. And here I was, shouting and shaking because someone had asked me to pass the salt!'

Debbie

The difficulty with stress also lies in the way it can creep up on us unawares. This is partly due to our non-stop involvement in a busy lifestyle that leaves little room for introspection; but it is also due to a side-effect of the stress itself. Just as adrenalin will slow digestion and speed the heart rate, so other hormones can numb our sensory feelings. This is very advantageous to someone hurt in battle or while fighting a wild animal – in order to save our lives we have to keep fighting, and therefore cannot be distracted by pain. It is only when we stop that we become aware of the amount of stress we are experiencing as well as the extent of the damage.

Psycho/physical Factors

Few of us know how to deal with stress. We hope that sleep or a good movie will help, or we pray that it will go away on its own, or that soon we will manage to get some time off. We get involved in mindless activities, play sports or watch television, thinking that this is relaxation. We invest an enormous amount of money and energy into making our appearance look stress-free; we worry that we will be liked or disliked, accepted or rejected. But does the new hairstyle or outfit really deal with the deeper issues of dissatisfaction, anger or fear?

Certainly psycho/physical stress can be temporarily eased by exercise, having a long hot bath or a gentle massage, or by going on holiday. However, how often do we end up having to deal with hungry mosquitoes, an over-loud disco or the air conditioning not working? Having a drink or watching a movie give us 'time off', as it were, but such activities do little to stimulate a real letting go or a release of the deeper causes of stress. If stress continues over an extended period it gets increasingly difficult to release the resulting physical tension and hormone imbalance, and we have to take more serious action.

> *'I was working in the business studies department of a university when I started having pains behind my eyes, like a dull ache. Then I had severe headaches, stomach pains and constant pounding in the chest. I would wake up tired and have to struggle through the day, unable to keep my eyes open. I couldn't sleep, and I became fractious and irritable. It got to the point where I resorted to psychiatric help – antidepressants, beta blockers, etc. – and long periods of sick leave. I was obsessed with the future and ruled by fear. Finally I began to take stock of my priorities and change my routine.'*
>
> David

Psychological stress throws us into completely chaotic states of mind in which our behaviour becomes irrational and unpredictable. We may be brilliantly clear one minute, only to find ourselves raging and angry the next. The effects can include depression, anxiety, addictive behaviour, loss of memory, disorganisation, poor self-care, neurosis or phobias. The chaos surrounds us, and soon it becomes impossible to find a clear exit.

Emotional stresses that arise are even harder to release. They include excessive anger or resentment, frustration, bitterness, jealousy, fear, panic and hatred. They dig deep into our psyche and affect us on a more unconscious level. This can lead to marriage problems, delinquent children, promiscuity and criminality. Simply going to the cinema or having a hot bath does not deal effectively with these problems. Counselling can help, but the primary need is to release the inner layers of tension, to go beyond the conscious mind.

The Relaxation Response

We often think of relaxation and meditation as quiet activities that lead to a passive and inactive state of mind. If you are living 'on the wire' it is easy to believe that you need to be stressed in order to function – that you would be too inert if you were relaxed, and therefore you would lack the necessary edge. However, there is a place where we are both alert and awake, yet completely relaxed at the same time. From this place we can act with great precision, but we do not become exhausted in the process.

The *relaxation response* occurs when we react to situations without an increase in blood pressure, heart palpitations or headaches, but are able to respond in an easeful and relaxed way, free of pressure. This is not the same as a passive or laid back attitude – a relaxed attitude can be extremely dynamic. For instance, when we are stressed any little thing can become an irritation until we finally lose our judgement or become angry. In a relaxed state those irritations do not build up inside as we are able to let them go before they arise, so there is no accumulation. Our judgement stays clear and we can act with awareness.

> '*Relaxation helped me to switch off my mind and release the tension in my body. Having achieved this I felt I could accept myself more fully. I feel myself lifting out of any moods or tiredness. I get recharged and reconnected and have a greater sense of self-authority. When I relax I concentrate on my breath and feel I am dissolving into my breath. Then my everyday problems dissolve and sometimes an answer to a problem will arise spontaneously.*'
>
> Helen

In a relaxed state all the psycho/physical impairments are improved. The blood pressure normalises and the heartbeat slows down; stress-related hormones such as adrenalin are not surging through the body; digestion and metabolism normalise; sympathetic nervous system activity is decreased, while the parasympathetic system is increased thus slowing heart rate and nervous activity; muscles relax; the body's facility for self-regeneration and healing is stimulated, as is the overall sense of sensitivity and wellbeing.

As the mind quietens and relaxes, fear, worry and the feeling of being overwhelmed decrease. The ability to concentrate increases, as do efficiency and clear-headedness. Emotionally we feel more stable and whole, less needy or demanding. Anger is decreased, as are possessiveness or rejection. There is a growing warmth, a sense of being more in touch with our true feelings. Life becomes something we want to participate in.

When we consciously relax or meditate, a level of peace and balance – a deep inner harmony – becomes possible. In a deeply relaxed state we emit what are known as alpha waves. There are four different levels of brain wave activity. Beta is the level of ordinary, day-to-day consciousness, when we are awake and active; if we start to get stressed, we go up high in the beta range. Alpha is the level we can reach when we enter into an inner quietness and the brain waves become calmed and eased. These alpha waves intensify through relaxation and meditation. Below these is theta, the lightly sleeping state, and delta, the deeply sleeping state. Entering into an alpha state can restore our balance and strengthen our whole system. This is not the same as just lying quietly – it is reached through consciously releasing the tension in the mind. True relaxation means going beyond the conscious mind. When we can relax in this way (and we are all capable of doing so), then our psychological, emotional and physical energy are balanced.

For example, during the practice of Inner Conscious

Relaxation the unconscious and subconscious patterns that have developed over years of suppressing tension are released. At the same time we are training the mind to relax so that further stress is not accumulated. By withdrawing from distraction and pressure we create a spaciousness in which we connect with a source of energy that is both revitalising and replenishing. Each time we relax we can connect with this source, like a well of healing. This enables us to begin the process of self-acceptance, developing a greater sense of inner ease. As this becomes an integral part of our day, so we develop self-esteem, a more positive attitude and an inner happiness. We start living more fully.

Spread Your Dhoti!

There is a feeling of tremendous breakthrough when a stressed mind gets to experience a state of deep relaxation. It is such a relief! It renews us on a very basic level. We feel more relaxed *with* ourselves, not just *in* ourselves. As there is less fear and more self-assuredness, we take a few more risks and jump in where we may have previously held back, whether through doubt or lack of confidence. We begin to see beyond the material pleasure/pain syndrome to a place of great joy. We start to live with dignity, fearlessness, basic goodness, kindness and insight. Most importantly, we stop needing to control so tightly, either ourselves or others.

Many of the relaxation and meditation techniques that we work with have come out of the spiritual teachings of yoga and Buddhism, both stretching back over 2500 years into the ancient traditions of India. There is a profound richness in these teachings as their purpose is to cultivate a genuinely peaceful attitude to life, to awaken us to our true happiness. India is a place of vast extremes, containing every possible facet of human existence. Yet it is this very rawness of life that has given rise to such great understanding.

On a recent visit to India we had tea with an American couple who have been running a clinic for disabled and handicapped children in Madras for twenty-five years. We found their sincerity and commitment to the suffering that surrounds them, and to the lifestyle that India demands, powerfully moving. But we could not help wondering how they had coped when confronted with the very different cultures and attitudes of India when they came from America in the early 1970s, especially as at first they lived in a mud hut with their four small children and few amenities.

'"During our early days I had been visiting a hill station when I had word that I was needed back in Madras – a bus and train journey away," Don told us as he stretched out his long frame on an old wicker chair. "The next morning, riding the bus down the mountain to the station, we unexpectedly came to a halt. A long line of traffic revealed an accident between a truck and a bus which was now blocking the road. I was concerned about catching my train so I began to try and organise a way through, unfortunately forgetting the legacy the English have left with the Indians – a great reverence of authority!

'There were buses stopped on both sides of the accident. "Could they not," I asked, "exchange their passengers, turn around and go back to where they had come from, taking the passengers that needed to get there?"

'"Oh no, sir," came the answer, "the buses are from different companies and so they would not be able to sort out the money for the tickets and we have no permission for this."

'Then I discovered one bus on each side from the same company! "Could they not exchange passengers?" I tried again.

'"But no, sir," said the drivers, "for then each driver would

end up at a destination where they were not meant to be, and there is no permission for this to happen."

'By now I had joined forces with a Swedish man who had a jeep. Together we worked out that if we could fill in the ditch beside the road then the bus could be moved back off the road on to the bank and there would be enough room for the cars to get past.

'"Oh no, sir," came the reply, "this is not possible. To fill in the ditch we would need permission, and we do not have the permission to do this."

'While all this had been going on, the various occupants of the many buses and cars now waiting on each side of the accident had spread their dhotis [long pieces of cloth tied around the waist] in the shade and were sitting or resting quietly. Eric and I were the only ones, getting very hot and irritated in the midday sun, who were trying to get anything done. Everyone else was quite happily letting events unfold by themselves.

'By now it was 1p.m. We decided that if nothing had happened by 2p.m. then we would fill in the ditch and move the truck ourselves! However, at 1.30p.m. the police arrived, assessed the situation, and gave the long awaited permission to have the ditch filled in and the truck moved. By 2p.m. we were on our way down the hill! I caught my train with quite a few minutes to spare.'

'"So how has India changed you?" we asked. "Has its innate spirituality touched you?"

'Don chuckled quietly. "Oh yes! If presented with the same circumstances now I would simply spread my dhoti in the shade like everyone else and let the situation take care of itself!"'

We remind ourselves of this story whenever we find we are trying to control a situation or are getting worked up about something. 'Just spread your dhoti', is like saying, 'Just relax, let go and let God.'

Climbing Upwards

Inside each of us is a place that is asking us to slow down, to make time to just be, time to spread our dhoti under a tree. It is as if our spirit is yearning to be free of the habits and limitations that keep us stuck and unsatisfied, like a flower that grows through concrete in its yearning for the light – a natural process fuelled by the desire for fruition, for completion. If we do not listen to that inner yearning we soon become alienated and disconnected from ourselves, locked into repetitive or habitual behaviour. To find deeper meaning and purpose in our lives and to shift some of the more stubborn patterns that limit our emotional and psychological freedom involves a process of undoing, of lightening the hold, of shifting our focus to a different goal.

'Low in the central brain lies the limbic system, where the aggression seems to start,' began an article by Lance Morrow in *Time* magazine. 'But there is a higher brain as well. If war originates as an impulse of the lower mind, then peace is an accomplishment of the higher, and the ascent from the brain's basement where the crocodile lives to the upper chambers may be the most impressive climb that humans attempt.'

To make this journey upwards from the brain's basement is the journey to our own fruition, the awakening of our sleeping Buddha. Well-tried and tested tools and techniques are available to help us. The impact that relaxation and meditation can have in our lives is vast and profound – it brings us home to our true self. What more could we ask for?

There is so much pain and suffering in the world – all around us we are confronted with homelessness, hunger, loneliness, arguments and fighting. But responding to that situation by suffering ourselves does not help resolve matters. A person who is stressed will create fear, anger, greed, loneliness and anxiety. We cannot give when we are in a needy place ourselves, nor can we really love or care for others when we do not love or care for ourselves. A person who is relaxed is able to love, to be generous and considerate, has space for others' needs and is selfless and tender. As we make peace with ourselves and our world, we are no longer afraid to give for fear we will go short, to love for fear we will be hurt, or to care for fear we will be rejected.

Deeply releasing the inner stress enables us to go from aversion or a longing for things to be different to an acceptance of what is; from being insensitive to others and only concerned with our own needs to being aware and considerate, seeing how we are all equally a part of the whole; from resisting change or feeling threatened by it to seeing the natural flow of all life. This journey is endearingly shown in the following letter, written by a prisoner in his early twenties to Sister Elaine MacInnes of the Prison Phoenix Trust: 'For as long as I can remember I've had a hurt, a pain inside, and since I came to prison it's got worse. So I cut myself or burn myself just to get the pain in a different place, on the outside .... I want you to know that after only four weeks of meditating a half hour in the morning and at night, for the first time in my life I see a tiny spark of something within myself that I can like.'

Practice – Just Being

Find a comfortable place to sit and close your eyes. Become aware of yourself. Bring awareness to your feet ... legs ... back ... front ... arms ... and head. Feel the flow of your breath. Feel your own presence. Experience the vibrance of the life force within you. Here you are: alive ... breathing ... sensing ... your heart beating ... your feet on the floor. Be present with yourself and whatever is happening, without judgement. Experience your insideness, your inner world, feel your body functioning and your lungs breathing. Watch your mind thinking. And just sit and be ... just sitting ... just being. Stay with this for a few minutes, or for as long as you like. Then take a deep breath and gently open your eyes.

Chapter 3

Turning Muddy Water into Sweet Milk

Have you ever thought how amazing it is that the lotus plant does not grow in a pure mountain lake but in murky mud and dank pond water thick with weeds, and yet its beautiful flower appears on the surface totally pure and pristine? Nature is astounding in its beauty and complexity. If we look closely we see that all life starts in the dark, either in the earth or in the womb, as the darkness contains the nourishment needed for life to emerge.

This is important to remember. It shows us how all the mud in our lives – all the difficulties, fears, concerns, doubts, insecurities, hurts, conflicts, everything that seems so impenetrable and difficult to wade through – is actually the very stuff needed for our growth. Without it we would have no ground, no strength, no nourishment. This is why we cannot push the darkness away or deny its presence. Conscious relaxation and meditation teach us how to find our nourishment from within, how to access a place that brings healing and wholeness, that embraces the darkness.

'On the day of my husband's funeral I was panicking. I felt unable to get through the day – it was too demanding. Finally I escaped from all the family milling around and went to sit alone in meditation in a quiet spot in the garden. Gradually I felt my fearfulness disappear, and a calmness and great strength seep in. There was a deep awareness that all I had to do was to reach into myself for what I needed.'

Margaret

The choice to either get stuck in the mud or to use it as nourishment and stimulation is always there: to let our lives go by in a dream, or to awaken with awareness; to wallow in self-pity, hopelessness, failure, lethargy and the longing for life to be different, or to find a deeper acceptance for things just as they are. Our ability to use the mud as our means for growth will determine the strength of our plant, for the stem of the lotus symbolises our intention and commitment – a pledge to our sanity, to our awakening. When our intention is inner peace and unconditional happiness we will slowly emerge from the mud, our roots always being fed by it, the bud of the flower heading for the sun. We need never be concerned about the flower opening for that will happen by itself as a natural response to the light.

Just as the stem uses the mud to produce a beautiful flower, so the transforming power that can take a difficult or even negative situation and turn it into something positive and uplifting is within us all. The Tibetans call it the power to turn shit into gold. A peacock eats poisonous snakes, yet transforms that poison into the beauty of its iridescent feathers. It is the irritation of a grain of sand that causes an oyster to make a pearl: no irritation, no transformation, no pearl. Can we not transform our own irritations – all the doubt, fear, anger or frustration – into pearls of wisdom?

'What is this nature?' asked Achaan Maha Dharma Tam, the gentle and stately monk who was so patiently guiding our retreat. 'Look at how the rain falls to the ground and makes muddy water. And how the coconut tree takes that muddy water all the way up its long, long trunk, to make sweet coconut milk. What is this nature that can take muddy water and make sweet coconut milk?'

Dare to Commit

For relaxation and meditation to have this effect in our lives it is essential that we make a commitment to practise. The world is like a magnet pulling our energy outwards to the objects of desire; now you have an opportunity to recognise and reverse that process, to discover the riches within. The commitment is to your sanity and freedom, it creates a spaciousness of acceptance that nourishes the spirit.

But there's never enough time! I have so much to do! The children are always too noisy/too demanding .... I have too many meetings/letters to be answered/orders to be filled/classes to teach/deliveries to be made ... the list is endless. Lack of time is the biggest argument against being able to practise – demands seem to fill our every waking moment until relaxation or meditation becomes our least priority. But perhaps this is more an expression of how difficult it is to make time in which to respect and appreciate ourselves. We have to stop and ask if we really *want* to change. Are you so used to being the way you are that it seems impossible to imagine being any other way? Do you feel validated by being needed and staying busy? Or do you even believe you are not the relaxing type, that if you do relax you will not be able to cope with the pressures you have?

No one can make time. No one can change your habits or routine. The commitment you make is not to anyone else – not to a teacher or even to your family – but is a commitment to living, for with this commitment you will find a deeper joy and happiness. The more effort you apply, the greater the opportunity for growth. That choice has to be made by each one of us. We can change the way we look, where we live, even who we live with, but unless we connect with who we are inside none of those external changes will make that much difference.

It is easy to feel guilty that the time you are taking to relax or meditate could be better used elsewhere. But because you are doing something for yourself does not mean it is selfish or even wasted time. Think about what happens when you do not make time for yourself, when your day is spent working or caring or simply being there for others. Do you get burnt out, resentful, irritated or even angry? Do you find stress building up? Do you lose your temper or get ill? Does the quality of care that you offer become affected by that inner tension? By taking time for yourself, by lowering your blood pressure and releasing stress, you are immediately creating a more harmonious environment with a greater ease and peace that can only benefit all those around you. When you are energised and feeling good you will be able to do far more than if you are dragging yourself through your day with little energy or in a bad mood.

When we take time out to focus ourselves it means we do not get so angry, resentful or frustrated; instead we have time to go within, to be quiet and connected. Then what we share with others is coming from that peaceful space. Is it selfish to spend time alone so that what you give to others is more genuine and heartfelt? Swami Satchidananda, Eddie's first meditation teacher, says that the wise ones are the most self-less, always giving and caring for others. But when it comes to their own peace they are the most selfish for they will allow nothing to disturb them. That is because they know that if their peace is disturbed they can help no one.

Taking time to relax or meditate is not the same as going for a walk or quietly listening to music. These are wonderfully relaxing activities, but they do not have the same effect as simply being still. Some people are fearful of stillness and keep distracted in order to avoid it, not realising that it is their resistance that is causing the fear, for when we let go into the quiet there is simply a greater sanity and sense of ease. Only half an hour a day can achieve enormous change which will help those around you as much as it does yourself. Others will find it easier to communicate with you, will enjoy being with you, will even be motivated to help themselves more.

So you really have to question your priorities. Do you want to be healthy and happy enough to work at it? Will you put time into it, even if it means getting up a little earlier or setting aside some time before you go to bed? Have you recently felt the earth beneath your feet, or noticed the smell of a flower, or the soaring of a bird in the wind? We discover beauty and joy when we let go of resistance and stress and reconnect with that quiet space within; when we discover the underlying essence of our existence rather than focusing on the details or the content. A stressed mind sees life as a burden or constraint, while a relaxed mind sees life as a challenge and meets it with dignity and fearlessness. The choice is yours.

Practice – Clarifying Priorities

Spend some time getting an overview of your priorities. Take a piece of paper and a pen. Settle your body and spend a few minutes just watching the breath and relaxing. Then slowly ask yourself the following questions and write down your responses:

- When does my life feel most meaningful, and how much time do I give to these meaningful activities?
- What are the least meaningful things I do, and how much time do I give to these activities?
- Is this how I want my life to be? Is it a true reflection of how I see my life unfolding?
- What qualities do I honour most, and am I embodying these in my daily activities?
- Do I consider peace of mind to be important, and how much time do I give to peaceful activities?
- How do I regard happiness? Do I want to be happy? Do I trust happiness? Do I believe I have to work for it or pay for it? Is happiness my birthright?
- What is stopping me from making happiness my priority now, in every aspect of my life?
- What one thing can I do or change to manifest my priorities?

Look carefully at your answers and recognise how you may be holding yourself back from happiness through fear, doubt or mistrust. See what changes are needed and how you can implement them. Try and find at least one thing you can commit yourself to doing that will generate greater peace, and then spend a few minutes looking at how the various aspects of your life might change if you did this one thing.

Content versus Essence

One of the reasons why inner peace and happiness are so misunderstood and seem so elusive is our tendency to identify with the content of our lives rather than the essence. We have many labels which identify our content: we are identified as English, Italian, Russian or whatever, depending on the country in which we were born; we each have a particular occupation, so we are identified as a teacher, therapist, gardener, cab driver and so on; we follow a particular religion or philosophy and therefore have an identification such as Jewish, Catholic or Buddhist. Beneath the big labels are the more intimate, smaller ones, such as recovering alcoholic, divorcee, asthmatic, homosexual, cancer patient, widow. Then there are personality labels like worried, angry, irritated, hopeless, coward, victim, martyr; as well as ways in which we think others see us, such as fat, skinny, loud, silly, thoughtless, dominating and so on. Note that most of the smaller labels we identify with are not very positive ones – we find it much harder to recognise and label our loving and caring qualities.

All these labels give us a sense of belonging and reason for being, they form our personal imprint. However, they are also a major cause of discontent. Our level of happiness becomes dependent on the content, and if that is not appreciated or satisfied the result is conflict or suffering. Look at the wars waged in the name of religion, the cruelty caused by racial prejudice – all because we regard the labels as more important than the person beneath them. We hold on to the content and make it our story, our personal saga; through it we gain recognition, prestige, sympathy and attention.

If the labels form our content, what of the essence? Who are we without the story, without the labels? Take a few minutes to think about this and try the exercise below. See if you can identify and then let go of your labels, of the ways by which you are known or which give a meaning to your life. This is a very valuable thing to do as it enables you to see that what you think of as the whole of you is actually only a

part. It also helps to identify and name your different person-
alities and to recognise them when they arise. Recognition
takes away their power.

For instance, we spent some time working with John who
had smoked pot for many years. He did not consider himself
an addict until he tried to stop. Even though he had never
smoked very much it had been reasonably consistent, and
now he was forced to be aware of how much his body craved
it, and how hard it was for him to face everyday reality
without it. Going through withdrawal was a painful process.
An immense longing to get high would well up and, as it was
not being satisfied, he would get angry, demanding and
rebellious. At first John did not know how to deal with this
– the longing and confusion were overpowering, attacking
all his normal sensibilities. He would have given anything to
get out of his head and away from the insistent voices.

Finally he decided to label what was happening, to name
it for what it was. He called this part of him Mr Addict.
Whenever the irritation, craving or inner demanding arose
he would call it by its name. 'I would say to myself, it's just
Mr Addict doing his rounds again. This gave me a spaciousness – I was able to maintain a sense of myself and not be
taken over by the power of longing. Most especially it helped
me to see that the addict was only a part of me and not the
whole of me.'

We are very attached to our labels and the story they
create, we introduce ourselves through our identifications,
and our lives are dominated by attachment to the details.
Seeing through this and being willing to give up our story is
no small step. 'There is such pressure to keep each of my
identities, each of my labels intact,' writes Joan Tollifson in
Bare Bones Meditation: Waking Up from the Story of My Life.
'Why do I feel as if no one really knows me until they know
my story? Tremendous fear arises at the thought of losing my

labels, and at the same time there is immense peace in living without them.'

Practice – Noting and Labelling

Take some paper and a pen. Take a moment to sit quietly, to breathe and relax. Then, down the left-hand side of the paper, make a list of all the labels you can think of that apply to you. See if you can put them in order, biggest first. Remember to include work, relationships, race, religion and age, as well as all the personal labels and ways you think of yourself, all the different aspects of your personality, and even ways you think other people label you. Write them all down. Then take a deep breath.

Now take each label in turn and imagine who you would be and how you would feel if you took that label away – if it was no longer you. See if you can find one word that describes how you would be without that label, and write it on the right-hand side of the paper opposite the label. For instance, without work you might feel free, so you would write 'free' opposite 'work'; or you might feel scared, in which case you would write 'scared'.

When you have taken away all your labels, have a look at the words on the right-hand side. What feeling is most dominant? Are there more words describing freedom or are there more describing fear? This is not a judgement, just a chance to see yourself more clearly.

Letting Go of the Labels

The practice of labelling will show you how attached you are
to your images, to your means of identification, to the
content of your story. What happens when you name these
parts of you? What is going on when you see them as having
specific characteristics and limitations? Can you see where
you are holding? Where are you willing to let go?

Labelling, or noting and naming, enables us to identify
what is happening before we become overwhelmed by it. It
gives us greater objectivity, most especially with the parts of
us that we most frequently seem to grapple with. By giving
each part a name we now know it and acknowledge its presence – it becomes more familiar and less fearful. 'Though it
may take a while to integrate noting into our daily experience, it eventually becomes a lighthearted recognition of
occasional heavyheartedness,' writes Stephen Levine in
Guided Meditations, Explorations and Healings. 'Nothing takes
us by surprise. We have explored our hindrances and we
meet them with the lighthearted ease of "Big surprise, fear
again, anger again, resistance again." Nothing becomes a
gentle acknowledgement of the passing show.'

Go further and see if you can find who you are without the
labels. What is left when you release your identifications,
when you put down your story? Who is there? Can you find
the part of you that is essence? In the stillness of meditation
we get to see the content, to note it and name it, while also
going further to release our attachment and touch into the
essence, into freedom. When we let go of the story we are
free just to be. For the labels represent only a part of us,
while who we are, deep down inside, is not the image or the
story. This is where true peace lies. What a joy!

Effecting Change

Shifting ingrained patterns of behaviour by releasing the labels and finding new and less destructive ways of relating is not easy. It feels safer to stay as we are, a built-in denial factor enables us to cope by blocking out much of our self-perception. When we are locked into a refusal to admit our reality, change becomes a threat rather than an exciting challenge or an opportunity for growth.

The reality of change makes us confront a deeper place inside, one that may not even want to be happy. This might sound ridiculous, for surely, given the option, we all want to be peaceful and at ease with life? But if we look closely at what we have invested in our present lifestyle we may find that it appears more important to us than does happiness. After all, if we become happy we can no longer maintain the 'Poor Me' syndrome, we will have nothing to complain about and no way of getting attention. Our ground will be different, our securities shifted. Unhappy or stressful circumstances do at least make us feel like everyone else – we are members of the Society of Moaners, we have difficulties to focus on, we have reasons for being unwell, unhappy, confused.

Change makes us take a new look at our belief in how fixed, immovable, solid or real we are. How often we have all heard words on the lines of: 'This is the way I am and I can't help it, so it's just too bad!' Holding on to how we think we are and our familiar patterns of behaviour is a strong defence mechanism, an important part of our ability to cope. If we saw ourselves in our true light – as temporary, constantly changing, very unsolid and unfixed – it would be difficult to generate the motivation to keep working so hard, to keep competing and struggling. Yet deep down inside we know we are only here for a short while. Every so often we get a glimpse of something very insubstantial and transparent, groundless and free. To integrate this awareness, in the face of life's demands and experiences, is not easy. Thus we create around us a solid, fixed world, one that supports our habits, patterns and rationalities and denies such formlessness.

Fear of change is fear of the unknown. Our present life may be stressful, demanding, perhaps lonely, but at least it is familiar, whereas change implies the unfamiliar, the untrustworthy. Who would we be? How would we behave? Would people still like us? Would we have the same friends? And would we still be able to cope? Change is a shift in the story line, a letting go of the known and a leap in the dark.

And yet change and impermanence are the very nature of existence – our thoughts, feelings and relationships are as changeable as the weather or the seasons, everything comes and goes. The natural world is constantly changing, each day offering something different, each season bringing its own rhythms. In resisting change we are resisting life; without change in ourselves we become locked into old ways. Integrating the reality of this is wonderfully liberating, like clearing away layers of dust and cobwebs to reveal a pristine beauty.

Jumping in Feet First

To make really significant changes can seem beyond our capability, for there are no reference points or familiar signposts. It takes courage to dance to the beat of our own drum, to step into a new place, to do things we never thought we could do. Your friends may think you are weird; your family may tease you. But a place of inner sanctity and serenity exists within each one of us, and your courage to connect with it will stir your sleeping Buddha into action, opening doors that have long stood closed and exposing a source of abundant richness and beauty.

'The crane was at the far end of the beach. Weaving our way through the hundreds of glistening bodies basking on the sand, I noticed the crane was attracting a lot of attention: something was happening there that was arousing both fascination and amusement. As we got closer I saw that it was in fact a bungy jump – 150 feet above us someone was getting ready to jump. We watched him fall, then bounce back and fall again, until finally coming to rest a few feet above the shoreline. "Not for me," I thought, simultaneously knowing I was going to have to do it, to confront myself in this way.

'So up I went. But when I got to stand on the edge of the platform ready to jump, a large rubber band attached to my ankles, my body wouldn't do it. There was no programming in my brain that knew how to deal with this situation. Deep within I knew I had to jump – to do something I didn't think I could do, to challenge myself in this way. But my body said "No" and my mind said "No". My inner spirit said "Jump" and my body stood still. Nothing connected. All the fear I had ever known was there in that moment. And I couldn't move.

'Below me voices started chanting: "Jump! Jump! Jump!" Even my instructor standing behind me was saying, "Now, Edward. Jump now." But I couldn't move. The minutes ticked by. And then I finally let go and dived into the unknown. It was exhilarating. It was wonderful. Most important of all, it released my fear. Sometimes we have to jump into the dark – with our eyes open – simply trusting that whatever happens will be right.'

Eddie

The Journey Is the Goal

By now you are no doubt becoming aware of a process, a movement, a journey that seems to lead from where you are towards a place ever deeper inside. In effect, this is a journey without end, even without a goal; rather it is a journey of continual discovery, with each discovery worthy of the entire journey. It is not the goal that matters but the travelling, the experience of the path itself. And although there are numerous paths described in every spiritual tradition, with detailed maps and signposts, we each still have to find our own way – we can never tread in another's footsteps, never walk someone else's path. At times we may get lost, or occasionally take a wrong turn. Sometimes we may wonder if we are even on the path at all. We may have to stop and ask for directions; or seem to make great headway only to find we are back where we started from.

In other words, the path is nothing if not adventurous. Despite clearly thinking that we know where we are going we can never see too far ahead, never know what lies in wait for us. Invariably we all experience similar conditions that demand, first, great trust, especially since we do not know what is coming next; second, enduring patience and fortitude, particularly when the landscape seems impassable or incomprehensible; third, unconditional acceptance in order to embrace everything we come across within ourselves; and, fourth, surrender to the great unknown.

Being on a journey of self-discovery can at times feel lonely, especially when we appear to be tramping alone across a desert. Why should we want to continue when everyone else seems to be having such a good time? Apathy and lethargy are familiar components of the path, as are times of struggle and doubt, confusion and lack of faith, as if we are in a dense undergrowth or thick forest. Yet once on this journey it is not easy to stop. Just as a plant will grow through concrete to get to the light, so our yearning for peace and unconditional happiness will urge us forward. At other times we will turn a corner only to find ourselves in a beautiful landscape, as if in a luxuriant garden or on a golden beach beside an endless blue sea. Like the forest, this too will pass, but such moments give us great strength to continue. They are moments of insight and awakening, turning points within ourselves that shift our perspective and open us to a different state of being.

By looking back over the terrain we have already travelled we can see how far we have come, the changes and shifts that have already happened, and how each situation contributed to us being here now. All those moments that seemed insignificant at the time did have meaning and were an important part of the whole. Who we are now is a result of our journey so far. Slowly we realise that the greatest journey takes place in just this moment, and that the more present we are the further we go, for this moment contains the whole journey within it.

Embracing Peace

Although we each have to travel our own path, at the same time nothing exists independently of anything else – there is an extraordinary inter-relationship between all things. We are intimately connected to each other, and from there to the whole, so despite our feeling alone we are actually always in association. Is the body separate from the breath? Is it separate from the food we eat? And is it therefore separate from the earth or the rain or the sun? Or the farmer or the shopkeeper? Or the tractor or the farm? We all walk the same earth and breathe the same air. We each want to find happiness and joy in our lives. And we are all in this together, just like the trees and animals. Can you find a single place where you begin or end? Can you find a single thing in the universe that is not a part of, connected to, or dependent on something else? Is not everything dependent on everything else?

Living without this awareness can lock us into a mental state where there is no room to breathe and no involvement with life: we are living only our small bit while shutting out the rest. In this place we forget the moon and the stars, the rhythms and impulses of life, the patterns of rain on a leaf, the sky at dawn, or the sharing of hearts. Awareness of our inter-dependence gives us a precious world to share, a place in the whole, a relationship of being.

What we think and how we behave constantly affects the whole, as we are all co-creators of our world; each one of us is responsible to each other and our contribution is vital. The greatest gift we can give to the world is our own peace – then at least there is one less person suffering. When we are balanced and at peace our contribution will be of real value and will not cause further conflict. If we are to encourage world peace we must first develop and experience our own peace, every day for the rest of our lives. 'Each breath we take, each step we make, each smile we realise, is a positive contribution to peace, a necessary step in the direction of peace for the world,' writes Thich Nhat Hanh in *The Heart of Understanding*. 'In the light of interbeing, peace and happiness in your daily life mean peace and happiness in the world.'

Practice – Extending Appreciation

Find a comfortable meditation seat as described on p. 137. Spend a few moments adjusting your body to get comfortable.

Now begin to develop a deep appreciation and gratitude for the cushion or chair you are sitting on, thanking it for supporting you in your practice. Honour the person who made your seat, and thank all the elements that were involved in the making of the different components.

Now extend your appreciation to the building around you, feeling gratitude for its protection and safety, for the space it provides in which you can meditate. Silently thank those who made the building, the materials they used and the work that was put into its construction.

Then extend that appreciation to the ground beneath you, always there supporting and sustaining you throughout your life. Feel a deep gratitude for this earth that sustains all life, that is a part of the intricate connection between all things. Feel a gratitude for the trees and plants, the animals and birds, the oceans and fish, all contributing to the whole.

Now extend your gratitude to your body, appreciating how it cares for and nourishes you, how it is within this body that you experience love, joy and unconditional happiness. Feel the vibrance and beauty of your physical self. Honour the way your body is dependent on the food you eat, the water you drink and the air you breathe. Honour the way it is clothed in fabric that started life as a plant or animal. Honour the connectedness of your physical body to all the elements of life.

Now extend that appreciation to your parents, for without them you would not be here, would not have this body, would not be sitting in meditation opening your heart to your true self. Honour however much or little they gave you as being the most that they were capable of. Now extend that appreciation further back, to your grandparents and distant ancestors. Between them all they gave you the colour of your hair, the shape of your eyes, the laughter in your voice, the form of your bones. They passed on to you their experience, their wisdom and insight, so that you may grow greater than them. Acknowledge that their bodies have now returned to the earth, completing cycles of inter-dependency, each feeding and nourishing each other.

From your ancestors slowly expand outwards, feeling your connectedness to all beings, in all directions. Honour the way in which we are all connected and inter-dependent. Feel how we all walk this earth together, breathing the same air, experiencing the joys and pains of life. See how within each one is a spark of light, sometimes ablaze, sometimes dim, but equally alight in all, each light reflecting all the other lights.

Now bring your appreciation and gratitude back to yourself and your breath. Become aware of the flow of your breath entering and leaving your body. We cannot own this breath: it is not ours to keep, but gives us life that we may share it. Spend a few moments appreciating your breath and the life it brings to you. Then take that appreciation with you into your daily life.

Chapter 4

The Lotus Blooms in the Sun

We already have peace inside us, it is not something that we get from elsewhere. We simply have to rediscover it, reconnect with it. But we are a bit like the musk deer that has a beautiful smell in its body, but searches the forest looking for that smell. We too have a beauty within us that is our nature – peace is always inside us, always available; it can never be found outside, no matter how far or wide we search. We just have to look in a different direction, and open our hearts and minds to a different way of being.

Ramana Maharshi, a great Indian mystic who died in 1950, made a delightful analogy with going to the cinema. He explained how, when we first go into the cinema, we see a white screen. Then the lights go down, the projector is turned on and the film begins. During the film, especially if it is a good one, we go through all sorts of emotions. We laugh and cry, we feel angry and joyful. Then, when it is all over, the lights come back on and we see a blank screen again. Ramana explained how our true nature, our real peace, is like that white screen upon which all the turbulent emotions of life get played out. But no matter what happens, that white screen is always there. It is the pure, untainted consciousness that is the substratum of all phenomena, our real self, ever peaceful.

Inner Transformation

The journey that brings us to this understanding – to the place where we are in direct contact with peace – begins with the movement from a deficient, weak or wounded self, the 'poor me' or 'help me' place, into a sufficient, strong and healed self, the 'I'm OK' place. Such a transition is the basis of spiritual development and is fundamental for wellness on every level. It may not happen quickly or even easily, yet it is essential to our development.

As a result of unhealthy childhood conditioning or a lack of emotional nourishment and support, a negative or wounded sense of ourselves often develops. The attitude of a deficient self has thoughts that say, 'I have been hard done by', 'I am always giving to others but nobody is giving to me', 'I am useless, I can't do anything right', 'Happiness is what happens to other people', 'My parents/family/children are to blame for my unhappiness', 'It's not my fault I'm like this', and so on.

Many of us come from this place to relaxation and meditation in the hope of finding release or healing. As we begin to practise, therefore, we may find that the focus is on healing wounds, on remembering and reclaiming those parts of our being lost in the past. 'In reclamation, we bring attention to understanding the painful conditions that created our weak, deficient, or barricaded sense of self,' writes Jack Kornfield in *A Path with Heart*. 'We reclaim our feelings, our own unique perspective, our voice that can speak what is true for us.' Through relaxation the inner stresses are released, while in meditation we develop greater self-awareness. In this way we can bring healing to the wounded self, and reconnect with our forgotten selves and lost voices.

As our understanding grows we begin to build a personal strength and inner wisdom, to develop tenderness, compassion, generosity and kindness. The attitude of a sufficient self affirms that, 'I appreciate and love myself as I am', 'I am responsible for my health and my psycho/physical state of being', 'I enjoy a flow of both giving and receiving' and 'I honour the truth within me'. This is an affirmation of ourselves just as we are, an acceptance of our human frailty within the framework of our human beauty.

There is an important difference between negating the ego or self and transforming it. When we negate or deny ourselves there is still a strong sense of 'I', of a me that is being denied or subdued. But when we transform the ego we go beyond any sense of separate self. To do this we first have to affirm the self – we cannot transform something we do not have. Only from a place of sufficiency and stability within ourselves can we begin to go beyond self-obsession and move into a more selfless and loving place. As Jack Engler, a Harvard psychologist, said, 'You must be somebody before you can be nobody.' To be genuinely selfless we first have to be selfish; from healing ourselves we are free to give to others.

We establish a healthy or positive sense of self by getting to know and make friends with ourselves. This means being open to seeing ourselves clearly, just as we are, without rejecting anything and without judgement, shame, guilt or fear. Acceptance does not mean we have to love everything – simply to see that everything is a part of us. The obstacles that confront us as we proceed – the dragons in the mind, the monsters under the bed, the bulls that charge from behind, the enemies on the battlefield – represent those parts of us that have been pushed away, as yet denied or ignored. To run from these simply increases our fear and resistance. We need to see how easily we get pulled into aversion and away from acceptance. How a deficient sense of ourselves can lock us out of our hearts.

'We must find in ourselves a willingness to go into the dark, to feel the holes and deficiencies, the weakness, rage or insecurity we have walled off in ourselves,' writes Jack Kornfield in *A Path with Heart.* 'We will see that each is made from a lack of trust in ourselves, in our hearts, and the world.' We will remain a victim of our own limitations until we can accept and honour who we are. Nothing should be unacceptable, no matter how unpleasant, ugly, or unlovable we think it is. Without acceptance, there cannot be change; from acceptance, love grows.

Flower Blossoms

As our relaxation and meditation practice deepens, the changes we experience are subtle and yet profound. With a healthy sense of ourselves we are able to develop greater kindness and sensitivity, a deeper level of perception. We are more aware of our place in the world; there is a greater sense of belonging, an inner security and strength. We see things just as they are in their own right, without any need of interference from us, and we are in consequence less vulnerable or easily influenced. There is a dignity and gentleness, an ability simply to be present and available, an openness to the shared human condition.

These effects are like the blossoms on a tree that give rise to sweet fruits. They indicate the growing awareness of ourselves in relation to others. When we are caught up in our own issues we cannot see beyond them, but now a bigger picture emerges that includes and responds to those around us. One teacher advised us to 'go behind someone' as if to embrace them and their understanding, so that we could be a friend, feeling what it was like to be them, feeling their feelings. Doing so widens the picture and enables us to step out of our ego-centred way of seeing the world.

As we connect more deeply with our own happiness, so we naturally begin to take joy in others' happiness, which in turn deepens our own. Such sympathetic joy is an integral part of the path. To be free with our joy means overcoming jealousy, competitiveness, judgement, comparison, prejudice, envy and selfishness – a long list of familiar feelings! Usually we take joy in others' sorrows, for it helps us feel better to know that someone else is suffering too. In our separateness we assess ourselves through comparison – we judge ourselves and each other on a socially acceptable scale of achievement. To feel joy that another is succeeding beyond our own achievements, has fallen in love or has something that we do not have, is to embrace ourselves with such acceptance that we do not feel we are lacking anything. It is a joyful resonance of passion for all life.

At the same time, it is equally important not to be glad when someone suffers who may seem to deserve it. No matter how atrocious an act may be, further suffering neither resolves the situation nor redeems our feelings. We cannot change the past, no matter what we do. But we can affect the future through our compassionate awareness, allowing love to embrace the pain, the open heart to embrace the fear. This is not to deny our anger or hurt in any way, but rather to see where we can be most skilful or altruistic in our actions.

The Dalai Lama always speaks of the importance to be

kind, to be generous of heart, that kindness is really all that the world needs to break down any differences or resistances. Such generosity of heart was seen in Nelson Mandela forgiving his prison warders after twenty-seven years in jail. It is seen in the father who forgave the IRA for killing his daughter. Ram Dass, the American spiritual teacher, told us that his altar held pictures of his guru and other holy men alongside one of the defeated Republican politician Bob Dole. This was not because he particularly revered the man, but because he realised that even Bob Dole was in need of being accepted and embraced, just as we all are.

Each one of us is capable of generosity, no matter how little we think we have. A smile is a great gift. Bringing joy to another by sharing ourselves is a great blessing. Watch those times when you feel mean-spirited, when you want to hold on to something even though you do not need it, or when you walk past someone in need of help. How does it feel inside? Does it make you feel good? And then spend a whole day practising generosity, a genuine sharing of your humanness, giving in whatever way you can. How does that make you feel? Then try doing it for a whole week.

Giving without any thought of getting is the most powerful act of generosity as it is unconditional, unattached, free to land wherever it will. But it can also raise fears about not having enough, about being ripped off, or about having to buy happiness. Watch where you are isolating yourself further through fear. And watch where resentment creeps in when you feel as if you are always giving but no one is giving to you. Are you really being generous? Or are you needing some acknowledgement or affirmation in return? True generosity has to include giving to ourselves, honouring our own needs, so that we are free to give to others.

Loving Kindness

As our awareness grows, the qualities of compassion, equanimity, patience and forgiveness develop. 'Metta' is the Buddhist term for loving kindness, the wish to see all beings happy and free from suffering. These are qualities to cultivate, and ones that arise naturally as the heart opens. In Pali (the ancient Indian scriptual language), *Metta* means both 'gentle' and 'friend', indicating how we can be a kind and gentle friend to both ourselves and others. This quality of friendship is described by Sharon Salzberg in *Lovingkindness* as 'A gentle rain that falls upon the earth. This rain does not select and choose – I'll rain here and I'll avoid that place over there. Rather, it simply falls without discrimination.' If love separates and judges then it cannot be love; for Metta to be authentic, it is through being a friend to all.

The meditation practice of Metta – the development of loving kindness (see Chapter 10) – begins with developing love towards ourselves before we begin to extend love outwards to our family, friends, and then to everyone else. This is by no means the easiest place to start. But the aim of this meditation is to develop love for all beings equally, to the point where we cannot say we love one person more than another, and in this we must include ourselves. This is true unconditional love, rather than a personal or subjective love. In this sense, loving ourselves is not an egotistic or narcissistic act but arises through deep appreciation of our humanness.

We consider it normal to love others even though we do not feel good about ourselves. Yet whatever we feel inside will be projected outwards – if a heart is closed to itself, how can it be open to anyone else? When we cannot embrace our own being, then the love we feel for others will be based on what we get from them – the affirmation and acceptance that we are not giving to ourselves. As we begin to generate metta towards ourselves we will see clearly where we feel undeserving or unworthy, how we find ourselves unlovable, or all the many ways in which we do not respect or honour ourselves. The meditation practice awakens mercy and kindness, enabling us to embrace and hold ourselves just as we are, with all our resistances and fears. In the arms of this love, loneliness is transformed into solitude, fear into respect, blame into forgiveness.

Many people find it hard to connect with their heart, to enter into the loving space at the centre of their being. It can feel as if the heart is closed, unreachable, as if we have built armour around it, a defence in response to the inner wounds of hurt, abuse, shame, loss or abandonment. Unconditional love is always present in the heart, but in the process of opening we may first encounter our defences. Normally we shy away from pain, doing anything we can to avoid it. But Metta cannot be developed by ignoring or bypassing pain. To work our way through the walls of resistance and hurt, to soften that armour and open the heart we need to welcome, enter into, and feel the pain. Let the memories surface. Let the tears heal the wounds.

Through relaxation and meditation, the contents of our wounded heart will come to us to be healed. Once we have felt and embraced them we do not need to hold on – they can be released, and they will go. The pain of our anger, fear, grief or loneliness does change, it does transform and heal. It also brings greater insight and wisdom. Pain and suffering crack open the ego so that the light can shine in; through humility comes grace.

Awakening Metta

The meditation practice of Metta is a wonderful way of opening to the power and depth of love. You may like to focus on just one stage of the practice at a time. For instance, try spending a whole meditation session just developing Metta for yourself. See if you can get beneath the resistances or reasons why you believe you are unlovable to a place that is accepting and appreciating. Love does not come immediately, it may take much practice before your heart slowly opens. Before love comes there needs to be an acknowledgement and an acceptance of what you find. Let there be mercy and compassion for past mistakes, for weaknesses or self-dislike, for all those parts that seem so unlovable. At the same time acknowledge your goodness, kindness and generosity, and celebrate your beauty. Develop an appreciation for your body, for your strengths and virtues. And let a deeper quality of loving kindness, gratitude and self-respect emerge.

At other times you may wish to focus just on a family member, a friend, or even someone with whom you are in conflict, and hold him or her in your heart as you focus on deep acceptance and loving kindness. As you do this all sorts of feelings may arise, especially ones of anger, frustration, irritation, guilt, shame or blame. The object is not to get caught up, whether in the emotions or in trying to understand them. Be objective, acknowledge these feelings, but keep going deeper into a place where you are identifying not with the personality but with the connectedness of your shared humanness. We do not have to have a reason to love.

As we accept our own pain we are more able to embrace that of others, whether close to us or unknown. We see clearly where actions are born out of confusion, defensiveness or fear. We can accept people's limitations and ignorance. In so doing, loving kindness naturally arises. Remember – we all make mistakes! We can see beyond the differences, beyond the place that focuses on the content, to the essence, the place where we all meet.

When we can extend our Metta to all beings, whoever and wherever they may be, we realise that it is not the individual we are loving, not the personality or the content that we are embracing, but the very essence of life: in just being alive, each of us is eminently worthy of love. We are not trying to fix anything, to change or heal anyone; we simply hold them and honour them and grow in love.

Finding love for just one thing naturally opens us to loving all. We do not bring in the love from outside – it is already inside and always has been; so Metta is a process of uncovering what is already there. That is what is so joyful about Metta – discovering the love already inside you, learning that in your heart you are love, that the pain or fear is only temporary. Beneath the fear is a depth of loving kindness, like a vast underground lake that is constantly nourishing and replenishing. As Leo Tolstoy said, 'There is only one task and that is to increase the store of love within us.'

Practice – Anytime Metta

This is fun to do. Try silently saying, 'May you be well' or, 'May you be happy' to each person you see or meet throughout your day. Spend one whole day doing this. It is important not to tell them – just feel it in your heart. You can do this to people on a bus, in a shop, at work, in the street or at home. Silently repeat, 'May you be happy,' when your partner or boss is upset or angry with you, or when someone is criticising you. Watch what happens inside yourself. Watch who you find it hard to love. There may be aversion, hypocrisy, ridicule or laughter but it will slowly become a genuine feeling.

As your heart opens, try silently saying, 'I love you' to each person. It will show you where you have resistance and even fear, but it will also connect you to your deeper feelings of love. If a day feels easy, try a whole week. Let it grow within you.

Compassionate Heart

With Metta arises compassion, a response of the heart to the suffering in others and in the world. Compassion is not a weak and passive state – we do not become doormats to be walked over. Rather, compassion arises with strength and tenderness, mercy and fearlessness. It is compassion that enables us to see ourselves just as we are and to witness the suffering of the world without shying away. Compassion is not pity, for that implies feelings of superiority and separation; rather it is a meeting of pain with love. We may not be able to alleviate suffering but we can be with it, be present and merciful, so that suffering is not endured alone.

Compassion also needs to be balanced by insight and wisdom, so that we can best judge the most appropriate or compassionate action. For instance, giving sweets to a starving child is not as appropriate as giving rice or fruit. Compassion urges us to respond to the suffering that we see, but wisdom sees beyond the suffering to what is really needed. Wisdom enables us to distinguish between things that are of real value and things that may simply be supporting an already unhealthy situation.

It is natural to feel powerless in the face of suffering, for it surrounds us wherever we look. But each one of us can make a difference. When we embrace ourselves with compassion, we have a greater capacity to embrace others. 'Do not make the mistake of thinking you are a powerless individual in a vast world,' writes Tai Situ Rinpoche in *The Way Ahead.* 'Know that you are armed with three great powers. You have the power of the body (the source of all action), the power of speech (the source of all expression), and the power of the mind (the source of all thought). Use them wisely and with compassion.'

Practising harmlessness is a form of compassion that can deeply affect our daily behaviour. Mahatma Gandhi lived by this, as does the Dalai Lama. Harmlessness, or *Ahimsa*, suggests we practise not just with others but also with ourselves. This means becoming aware of all the subtle ways in which we put ourselves down, dislike ourselves, stress our bodies or minds or limit our potential; as well as the ways we treat others, criticising or finding fault with them, feeling superior, causing pain or grief. Ahimsa reminds us of our basic humanity, our shared humanness, the fact that beneath the differences we are all in this together. It puts compassion into action.

Ahimsa is the intention to live with gentleness and awareness. In many ways it is not possible to live without causing some level of harm, but it is our intention, the focus in our hearts, that makes the difference. If we see each being as a reflection of both ourselves and of the whole, then we will not be abusive or uncaring but will respond with love.

Opening to Forgiveness

Forgiveness is very close to compassion and loving kindness. In practice it is hard to separate them, for an open heart cannot hold on to rage, revenge or guilt. Forgiveness arises unbidden when we enter into love.

Focusing on the possibility of forgiveness immediately confronts us with where pain, anger or hurt reside. It is important to acknowledge this, to feel the anger, to accept our hurt and not to deny these feelings in any way. Forgiveness does not mean a repression of pain, nor does it mean to forget; it is not a denial of suffering. We need to see clearly what is there, to experience the depth of our fragility or rage, our shame or blame. However, we also need to see how pain from the past keeps us locked in, unable to be emotionally free, how we become a prisoner of our own resentment, anger or guilt.

It is vital to realise that forgiveness does not mean we have to forgive the act, which may well be unacceptable or unjustifiable. We need to see the act for what it is, while also seeing the person behind that act, and in particular the pain or ignorance that influenced them to behave as they did. This does not mean that we should ignore or forget the intensity of feeling, the hurt or abuse that was perpetrated. But we can forgive the person through recognising their fear, their inability to see what they were doing, their own pain. This also applies to ourselves – to the hurt we may have inflicted on others in response to the pain or anger we felt inside ourselves.

Brigit came to one of our workshops. She was desperately trying to forgive her brother for abusing her as a child but had so far been unable to get away from the image of what he had done to her. Now, in meditation, she visualised him and saw his acts of atrocity as a dark and formless shape that she took out of him and put on one side. Then she turned back to her brother and saw him as he was, locked in his own pain and conflict. Finally she was able to open her heart and her forgiveness to him as a person, emersed in his own confusion.

As we enter into a willingness to forgive, there comes a place where we have the choice of staying with the story –

identifying with the content and holding to the pain – or opening to forgiveness. To forgive means to let go of the rage, resentment and shame; it means there is no longer anything to be attached to, no more reason for our suffering. Do not expect this to happen quickly: there may be many layers of emotion to go through, many memories to be uncovered, feelings of tremendous guilt, or the desire for revenge, or waves of anger may need to be released first. But it does mean that we have the chance to free ourselves of this emotional weight, this burden of pain. We can put down the story, the identity we have carried for so long.

The beauty of forgiveness is that it takes away the power that others may have over us. As long as we continue to feel hurt, hard done by, angry or abused, then the abuser still has power over us, limiting our ability to give emotionally, to trust others, to love freely. Forgiving lets all that go. It has nothing to do with anyone else; it does not matter if the other person does not even know, for the forgiveness is within our own heart. Forgiveness is the gift to ourselves that we no longer wish to carry this pain or to give our power away. And with forgiveness comes a great release: we are free to love, cry, to laugh and dance again.

The forgiveness meditation (see Chapter 10) enables us to release our attachment to the pain and accept our human frailty. As with the Metta meditation, it begins with forgiving ourselves. This is certainly the hardest place to start, but very often when we have been hurt or abused there is a place inside us that blames ourselves or believes we must have done something wrong to deserve such pain. For us to forgive anyone else we must forgive ourselves – for believing we were wrong, for bringing hurt to another, for abandoning ourselves, or for treating ourselves with disrespect and disregard. We also need to feel forgiveness for feeling rage or anger towards someone else.

When we are able to forgive ourselves for those times we have hurt either ourselves or another, it is easier to forgive someone else for hurting us. When we see how we can cause pain, how easily our own anger can spill over, or how our insensitivity can dominate our behaviour, then we can recognise the same in someone else. Have you ever noticed how, when you are in a good mood, you will spend fifteen minutes trying to get a small spider out of the bathtub, but when you are in a bad mood it is much easier to turn on the taps and flush it down the plughole? Can you recognise that same behaviour in an angry exchange between two people?

Forgiving others comes as a reflection of our own forgiveness. Have patience – such forgiveness does not come immediately. Great anguish may be uncovered, sorrow or betrayal may need to be released, a deep shame or grieving or sense of abandonment felt in the heart. Be gentle and loving, kind and caring with yourself.

From here the practice moves into bringing forgiveness to someone who has harmed or hurt you. To begin with you may want to choose a person who has only hurt you a little, leaving greater hurts for when you feel more open and more easily forgiving. There is no rush, go gently. It is very important that you feel ready to forgive, so you are not just paying lip service. And do not look for miracles, change may come slowly and subtly. Many different feelings may arise as you go into the meditation; let them have a voice and embrace them in your love.

In the final part of the meditation you ask forgiveness from those whom you may have harmed or hurt. Although they are not present, in the meditation you can release the guilt and shame you may be carrying. It helps to see that you are no longer the person who did these things, just as anyone who has hurt you is no longer the same person. We can ask for forgiveness for who we were then. As much as we need to give forgiveness, so we also need to be able to receive it, to welcome it into our hearts, to be forgiven and to put down the pain. So often what we forgive in another also needs to be forgiven in ourselves. When we forgive both ourselves and others, there is a healing spaciousness.

No Boundaries

'As the last meditation session of the evening drew to a close, the sky suddenly opened, monsoon rain cascading down like a waterfall around us. Silently, we gathered at the entrance to the hall, sitting on the steps under the overhanging roof, candles brightening the darkness, reflecting a soft light on drip-ping leaves, the sound of the rain highlighted by our own stillness. Where were the boundaries, the separations? Where was the difference between the leaf and the candle, the reflec-tion and the flame? Where did the rain end and I begin?'

Debbie

Inner peace arises from the very depth of our being. It is a true coming home to a place which we always sensed was there, sometimes glimpsed but rarely stayed in for long. Through relaxation and meditation we have the chance to let go of what is stopping us from being free and to sink into the softness of peace, like rain into soft earth. The various practices in this book are there to show you that beneath the struggle, confusion, doubt, fear and insecurity there is a place that is still, that is constant, that is love. That place is revealed when you put down the labels and identifications, when you let go of the story, when you step through the boundaries. When you just are. Being still. Then your sleep-ing Buddha will begin to arouse and stretch.

Practice – Healing Heart Meditation

This meditation brings healing through the heart. Begin by finding a comfortable sitting position, as described in Chapter 9. Close your eyes. Feel relaxed and at ease with yourself. Let all thoughts of the day fade away.

Become aware of your physical body ... experience your whole body ... repeat silently to yourself three times, 'I am aware of the whole of my body.' Visualise your body as if it were a temple. You are in this temple your whole life. Know that it is a blessing, a gift you have received with deep appreciation and thankfulness. It is in this temple that healing takes place, a healing that brings you closer to yourself, your peace, the love that is within you.

Now become aware of your breath, of the incoming and outgoing breath. Feel that your breath is your best friend, always there for you. Get closer to your breath. Become more familiar with this friend. The closer you come to your breath the greater the inner feeling of peace, like a close friend who knows you well. If thoughts come into your mind see them as if they were birds in the sky and let them go.

Now focus your awareness at the heartspace in the centre of your chest. Breathe into this space, breathe into your heart. The heart is unconditional love that supports your whole being, nourishing your whole body, embracing you completely. Breathe into your heartspace and let that feeling hold you. Breathe out any tension.

Your heart is like a flower opening and loving. Visualise in your heart a red rose – see the petals and the colour, smell the fragrance. Feel the rose opening as you breathe into your heart, softening and releasing any resistance. Know that you are love, that your true nature is pure loving energy.

Embrace yourself in your heart. Hold yourself in your heart gently and tenderly, and feel any tension softening and dissolving. This love is healing you. Silently repeat to yourself, 'May I be well, may I be happy, may I be healed.' Release any resistances that may arise, any reasons why you should not be well, any feelings of not being worthy of happiness. Keep breathing into your heart, feeling this love for yourself as if you are a beautiful flower.

Your love is your healing energy. Feel that love connected to universal love, to divine love, supporting this whole universe – the earth that is in orbit, the trees, the oceans and seas, the stars and the sky. Through your heart you are one with the universe. As you love yourself the universal love will fill you and nourish you.

Silently repeat to yourself, 'My body is my temple. My breath is my friend. My mind is calm and peaceful. My heart is loving. I am pure love.' Feel in your heart that you are one with universal love. Silently repeat three times, 'I am being healed by love.' Know that your love is a gift to be cherished. Treasure yourself always. It is love that heals. Feel the peace and the joy of this love.

Gently come back into your breath, your body and the room you are sitting in. Let this love be for the benefit of all beings. Take a few moments before you move. Feel the love within you shining in your smile.

PART TWO

RELEASE, RELAX, RENEW

Chapter 5

Letting It All Go

Having explored some of the characteristics of the journey, let us now enter the environment in which our journey takes place. In this second part of the book we shall explore the many aspects of relaxation. This chapter looks at the various requirements and any difficulties you may encounter. Chapter 6 offers a more detailed description of the practice and longer instructions for practising; while Chapter 7 explores the realm of creative visualisation. It is important to remember that relaxation should be developed before meditation, for when we are relaxed and at ease our meditation practice is more beneficial and effective.

'Relaxation has helped me to clear my mind and get my priorities right, has helped me to develop a centre of tranquillity within myself to cope with problems that arise in my life. That doesn't mean to say that I don't get upset, or cross, or panicked. I'm the same as anyone, but now I can take a few

deep breaths and distance myself from the problem for a while and then deal with it in a calmer state of mind.'

Dorothy

It does not matter what state you are in when you come to practise Inner Conscious Relaxation. You need not be concerned if you feel uneasy, distracted, full of anxiety, or psychologically or emotionally off balance. You can begin wherever you are at within yourself. ICR is neither a meditation nor a concentration, and your mind is not being controlled or changed; it is simply a practice of awareness. It is not a means of self-analysis but a way of emptying or letting go and realising the source of our own peace. During ICR all of our faculties are present – we are fully awake and not under the influence of anyone or anything. ICR takes place inside of us, in the inner space between sleep and the external world.

Everything we have ever experienced is imprinted in the mind. As the relaxation becomes more profound we go deeper and release the hold of past experiences. We do not have to relive or even remember these experiences in order for the tension caused by them to be released. ICR is a very gentle and loving technique. The benefits come as a greater ability to cope, to be at ease no matter what is going on, to be truer to our feelings and less likely to fall into habitual responses. ICR brings us closer to ourselves and enables us to know ourselves more intimately. Remember that beneath any unresolved issues is your peace – it is always there.

How Long and What Time?

Start with the Instant ICR on p. 78, taking just ten minutes a day. As you get more comfortable with that, move on to a longer practice of thirty minutes, as described on p. 85. You may find you can only manage a longer practice once a week but can maintain ten minutes per day for the rest of the week, or you may prefer to do ten minutes twice a day. After a few weeks of practising ten minutes once or twice a day, try a whole week of doing thirty minutes every day so that you can really experience the benefits of longer practice.

Be gentle but firm with yourself. It is best to practise every day if you can, but if this is not possible or is going to put too much pressure on the rest of your life it is just going to end up creating more stress, which is pointless. Make a commitment to practise as often as you sensibly can and draw up a schedule that you feel you can fulfil without causing difficulties elsewhere in your day. Even if you can only start by making a commitment to practise for fifteen minutes once a week, that is better than not doing it at all. Every time you practise will help. You have to decide that you want to do this more than anything else, so that it becomes a priority and not the last item on your list of things to be done. The more you do, the more you will benefit; the less you do, the less you will benefit. It's that simple. No one can make you do it, no one can do it for you.

In the same way, decide what time of day works best. Finding the right time to practise is as important as the practice itself. You cannot hope to have a quiet and meaningful experience if you try to practise at a time when the children are running riot around the house, when meals need to be prepared, when you have deliveries waiting to be made or meetings to be attended. You have to be realistic.

Are you a morning person or an evening person? Do you wake up alert and ready to go, or do you take your time to wake up? If you come round slowly in the morning, practising ICR at that time would probably send you straight back to sleep! But if you are more alert then you may find the early morning the best time as it will set you up for the whole day. If you have a quiet space during the day – perhaps if you are at home when the children are at school, or if you have a place where you can be alone at lunchtime – you may prefer to practise at that time.

Alternatively, early evening can be excellent because practice at this time eases and releases the stress built up during the day. You may want to do some simple stretching exercises first to release any physical tension in your muscles. Then again, if it is more practical you may prefer to practise later in the evening when you can have half an hour to yourself, or even before you go to bed. The time of day is up to you.

What is important, once you have found the right time, is to stick to that time and set it aside on a daily/weekly basis. This implies being committed to what you are doing and imposing some discipline upon yourself. Your mind will come up with numerous reasons why you should not practise and all sorts of urgent things that you must do now. But if you have already committed yourself to doing your practice at this time, let the other things wait. Obviously there may be occasions when you really cannot stick to the regular time. When this arises, you have to accept that this week/day is going to be different – just return to your routine as soon as you can.

Discipline is actually very liberating. When we make the commitment to practise and discipline ourselves to fulfil that commitment it creates a space in which we do not have to keep re-making the decision. Bringing more discipline or order into our lives is a way of generating respect both for ourselves and for those we live with. When there is order there is spaciousness and freedom; without it there is chaos and we soon become immersed in confusion. Creating a time for our practice and maintaining that commitment is the beginning of creating real self-respect. Both the mind and body respond to a routine: the memory of each previous experience enables you to settle more quickly into the practice and release any disturbances. There is a sense of continuity and rhythm.

Posture and Place

Where you practise is also important. You need to find a place where you can be undisturbed, quiet, warm (but not too warm or you will soon fall asleep), and where, preferably, you can lie on the floor (or on a bed if necessary, but again this can soon have you sweetly snoring). If it is uncomfortable or difficult for you to lie on the floor, or you are not in a place where it is possible, do the relaxation sitting in an upright chair; but it is preferable to lie down, so that your body can completely release any tensions. Put a blanket or rug on the floor and have a light blanket to cover you. When you relax the body slows down and can cool off a little, so it is important to stay covered in case of draughts. Put a small pillow under your head if you like.

Wear loose, comfortable clothing. Undo any belts, and remove glasses, watches and any jewellery that might become distracting. When you turn your attention inwards it is important not to have anything in the vicinity that might pull your energy outwards. Remember to turn the telephone off and/or switch the volume down so that it does not bother you. If you think other people may be around, leave a note on the door to explain what time you will be available again. That way they will not have to disturb you to ask you when they can talk to you!

Making these arrangements is a part of your mental preparation – a way of saying yes, this is my time, just for me, and it is my commitment to my own sanity and peace. When you have made your schedule and arrangements, stick with them despite any opposition or resistance. Very soon both you and everyone around you will come to acknowledge that this time is for you alone.

Variations on a Theme

The practice of relaxation need not be limited to a full half hour lying on the floor. That is the most valuable form, especially over a long period of time, but you can also practise at any time, anywhere, for whatever length of time you have available. Short sessions here and there are invaluable additions to your normal practice. They also give instant relief from mounting tension, helping you to cope with all types of stress-producing situations.

If there is nowhere for you to be alone, a toilet or bathroom makes a wonderful place to relax! For instance, you can disappear into the nearest gents' or ladies' room and simply spend a few minutes sitting quietly with your eyes closed, watching your breath. You can do either of the practices described on pp. 12 and 29 until you feel calm and relaxed; or try the instant ICR at the end of this chapter.

Even if you cannot be physically alone, you can still practise. If you travel to work by train every morning, use that time to relax, even in the midst of other commuters. It can be done if the will is there. Alternatively, find a garden or park to sit in away from the main stream of people walking past. If you are at your desk, can you shut the office door and be undisturbed for fifteen minutes? Just close your eyes, let your focus go inwards and become aware of your breath; systematically work your way through each part of your body, relaxing and releasing; then repeat 'soft belly' for ten breaths

– more if you have time. Or use your coffee break time to focus mindfully on your breathing and relax every part of your body. If you are at home you can do it while the children are busy with some activity that does not involve you. Even a few moments will make a big difference. Breathing with awareness brings you closer to yourself, closer to your peace.

A word of warning: just do not do it if you are driving a car! On no account should you play relaxation tapes or close your eyes to focus on your breathing if you are in charge of a car or any other piece of machinery. If you are driving and feeling tense, simply deepen your breathing into your belly and silently repeat 'soft belly, soft belly' to yourself, while keeping your eyes open. You can do the same with any part of your body that feels tight. Take your focus of attention to your shoulders, neck, legs or arms and breathe into that part, silently repeating 'soft shoulders' or which ever part it is. You can watch the flow of your breath while your eyes are open, consciously focusing on the breath so that your mind has a chance to be quiet. If necessary, pull off the road to practise more deeply. Being relaxed while you are driving, especially over long periods, is very important. Then when someone cuts you up and gives you the finger, you won't feel road rage welling up inside but will be able to laugh it off and wish them well!

Stressful situations can happen at any time – from a baby waking too early and crying too loudly, or a car splashing muddy water all over you as you wait for a bus, to an angry boss telling you off for something you didn't do, or a long queue at the bank which means you miss your train. How we respond to these situations is up to each one of us. Understanding relaxation more deeply and knowing how to practise by just watching the breath for a few minutes is like having an instant anti-stress toolkit. It enables you to enter into a peaceful state no matter what is going on around you. Remember, happiness does not come from outside but is the result of your inner attitude.

The Distracted Mind

'When I first started relaxation I could not let go. My mind was going at a rate of knots. I felt I had a lot of jumbled up wires in my head, or even a bird's nest! I kept saying, "I must relax", "I must relax", which just made it worse! Now I am much calmer. I can look back and laugh at how tense I got trying to relax.'

Freddie

Relaxation practice is there to help you, to enable you to let go and release the obstacles to your peace and happiness. So if you are getting tense or worried about finding enough time to do the practice, or chastising yourself because you simply lie there thinking about other things the whole time, or get upset because you missed doing it one day, then your attitude is self-defeating. You are practising relaxation in order to help yourself, not to build up more tension. You need to be gentle, respectful and grounded in your approach.

The difficulties most commonly encountered during ICR are increased tension, distracting thoughts or falling asleep. Very often it is our longing to let go that actually increases the tension just when we are trying to relax. The challenge here is to stop trying while continuing to practise. The tension is due to the mind creating a fear of not being able to relax, so by focusing on the words of the instructions (easiest if listening to a tape or in a class) your mind will be distracted from creating more tension. You do not have to try to relax – just listening to the words and following the instructions will make relaxation

76

occur. The more you do this the easier it will get, and suddenly you will find that there is no more resistance – you have been relaxing without noticing it.

Thoughts are bound to come and go because the mind creates dramas, stories and fantasies that easily engage our attention. The whole reason we are relaxing is to help us calm the mind, but we cannot do this forcibly, just as we cannot catch the wind or stop the waves. What we can do is move with the wind or flow with the waves. This means surrendering to the instructions. Always use the breath to relax the body, and the instructions to relax the mind. Whenever you become aware that you are thinking or getting distracted, simply return to the practice. And do not give up hope – practice soon pays off in increasing your ability to quieten and focus.

'When I am feeling very restless I cannot relax easily. Thoughts keep distracting me. I have learnt to go with this feeling more now and not feel so frustrated. The less I resist the more I relax. During the best moments, I experience a deep sense of calm which has a spiritual quality. I feel at such times a great sense of the oneness of creation – oneness with noises outside the window or thoughts that drift in and out of my mind. When I am fully relaxed there is no separation.'

Steve

It is quite natural to fall asleep during relaxation, as ICR takes place in that space between sleep and wakefulness. The way to stay awake is through concentrating on the instructions. If you really listen and follow the words, your mind will stay focused. Or try practising at a different time of day – vary the time so that your body rhythms are changed. Doing some stretching, dancing or jogging before you relax is a great way to stay awake as your body will be fully energised.

And if you do sleep, then enjoy the rest!

Deep relaxation is as important for our waking time as it is for our sleeping time. We need to release the stress that accumulates so that our sleep is deep and restful. When we are locked into a stress-creating syndrome our sleep is often restless and shallow and does not satisfy our needs, leaving us tenser than when we started. ICR can therefore be used to help insomnia. Do the practice in bed, with the hands facing palms downwards rather than palms upwards (as in the normal practice); it will help you to relax deeply and let go, so that sleep comes by itself. Chances are that you will fall asleep before the practice is finished.

Practice – Instant Inner Conscious Relaxation

(10 minutes)

You can practise this anywhere – at work, sitting on a park bench, at home, even on a train. Start by finding a comfortable place to sit or lie down where you will not be disturbed. You may want to play some very gentle, quiet music. If you are sitting, try to use a straight-backed chair and have both your feet flat on the floor (not crossed) and your hands on your thighs, palms upwards. If you are lying down, have your feet slightly apart and your arms by your sides, palms upwards. You may want a light blanket to cover you. Close your eyes.

Begin by becoming aware of the rhythm of your breathing. Just watch the movement of the breath as it enters and leaves your body. Start to feel yourself relaxing as you breathe – breathing out tension on the out breath, breathing in ease on the in breath. Watch and count for ten breaths.

Now bring your awareness to your right foot. Tighten the muscles, hold, then completely let go and relax your foot. Do the same with your right calf: tightening, holding and then releasing. Now the right thigh: tighten, hold and release ... then the left foot ... left calf ... and left thigh. Both legs are now relaxed and at ease. Breathe into your legs and feel them letting go. Now go to the right buttock and the left buttock: tensing, holding and releasing. Work your way up the whole of your back: the lower back ... middle back ... upper back: tighten, hold and release, letting go. Keep breathing.

Now the lower abdomen ... the midriff ... the chest. Then move to your right hand ... lower arm and upper arm ... right shoulder. Then the left hand ... lower arm ... upper arm and left shoulder: tensing, holding and releasing. Now both arms are completely relaxed and letting go. Breathe into both arms. Now move to your neck ... relax all the muscles in your face ... and then the whole of your head. Feel your whole body relaxing, releasing, letting go.

Repeat silently to yourself, 'My body is released and relaxed ... my heartbeat is normal ... my mind is calm and peaceful ... my heart is open and loving.' Repeat this three times. Then bring your attention to watching the flow of your breath for a few minutes. Let yourself sink into the natural rhythm of the breath as it enters and leaves your body. Do not try to change your breathing pattern – just move with the natural flow of your breath.

Now visualise yourself sitting on a beach, the heat of the sun warming your back and the sound of birdsong in your ears. Feel the rhythm of the waves as the rhythm of your breath – the in and out flow – for this rhythm is the rhythm of all life, the rhythm of the universe. Become one with this rhythm for a few moments, let it flow through you.

When you are ready, let the visualisation fade, take a deep breath and let it out. Become aware of your surroundings, then gently open your eyes and have a good stretch.

Chapter 6

How ICR Works

ICR begins by relaxing the body mentally. We then bring awareness to the breath. The rhythm of the breath has a relaxing effect and is an easy way of focusing the mind. If your mind drifts at any time, just return to the breathing. Breath is like home base. It internalises your consciousness and brings you into the present moment. The mind has the tendency to jump from thought to thought and can easily be distracted, so your breath is like an anchor to keep your mind focused in one place.

Rotation of Consciousness

Awareness follows a rotation of consciousness through the various parts of the body. This enables you to mentally relax and gently withdraw your mind from the pull of external stimuli. Bringing awareness to each part of the body creates a relaxation response in the corresponding part of the brain.

Through the brain you link or connect the body, mind and emotions – when they are in harmony your system is working at optimum efficiency. The rotation of consciousness through the body systematically relaxes parts of the brain that you are normally unable to reach. As you move through the body, silently repeating the name and visualising each part as you bring your awareness to it, you will begin to feel more comfortable and tension is released. You are setting up a network of communication throughout your whole being.

Sensations

Then the practice moves to experiencing the opposite sensations such as heaviness and lightness, or hot and cold. This is to achieve a balance between your inner and outer environment. As you create the feeling of heaviness you are sending a message to the brain to release even more of its tight hold or tension. To become heavier and sink into the ground creates an emotional relief: it takes the pressure off the various muscles, tendons and joints. There is no need to hold on – you just sink into the ground and it naturally takes you deeper. Then you create the feeling of lightness, a sensation of softness and floating away. Here you begin to see your experience in an objective rather than a subjective way, and there is a sense of detachment and freedom.

Visualisations

After relaxing the different parts of the brain and body you bring your awareness to the area of your heart and create a series of visualisations. By staying with the various images in the practice you move through layers of impressions in the conscious and unconscious while remaining undisturbed. In this way you bring the conscious mind into the unconscious and can release the hidden, more repressed tensions – the deeper layers of stress – giving access to a great reservoir of energy. The images are loving and healing, acting as a catalyst to focus your attention and create an environment of openness to unconditional happiness.

ICR is not a practice of concentration but an unbroken awareness that uses images and symbols to draw you into a deeper state of release. You are simply the witness, so do not judge or resist what takes place, just observe. The more relaxed you are, the more freely and clearly will the images come. The visualisations take place in your heart; if this is difficult, simply hold the images in thought form.

At times spontaneous visualisations, colours or sounds may arise. Through the images you are bringing the waking state into the unconscious, enabling a profound shift of tension to take place. Your collection of hidden impressions, feelings, traumas and memories is accessed; relaxation is essential to bring healing to these deeper levels of your being. By simply observing whatever arises and staying with the practice, the ego does not get drawn in or attached, and so any trauma is instantly released.

The Resolve

At both the beginning and the end of the practice you make a resolve or *sankalpa*. In life we make many resolves – perhaps to try to change bad habits and to cultivate good ones, such as to be more honest, to lose weight or to be kinder. Somewhere in our minds we want to get it right, but it often feels as if we are controlled by hidden or unconscious desires that pull us away from such good intentions.

This is why the resolve or positive affirmation is so important. Creating a resolve is a way of redirecting your life to flow in a healthy and loving direction. What you put into your mind when you are in a state of deep relaxation will take root like a seed being planted in a garden. You are opening yourself to real change. Tiny seeds grow to produce beautiful fruits. The resolve you make at this time will come to fruition.

Creating a resolve means focusing on your deeper purpose, your highest aspirations. It is more than just desiring to give up a bad habit – it is what gives your life real meaning, what inspires you most profoundly. It will enable you to release whatever is holding you back and will give you strength and guidance to go forward. As you make a resolve you may well encounter resistance, doubt, cynicism and insecurity. Each time you practise ICR you use the same resolve until it feels well rooted, so it is important to believe in your resolve, to create one that feels right for you. Here are some suggestions: use them as ideas to find your own.

- 'May I be an instrument of compassion and loving kindness.'
- 'May I awaken to the truth of my being.'
- 'I resolve to treat all beings equally with love and respect.'
- 'Unconditional happiness fills my being.'
- 'I honour the God in myself and in all beings.'

The resolve will slowly influence your behaviour to bring about a deeper level of transformation. Remember, all these things take time. You may have spent many years accumulating tension and fear, so it will take a while to reverse this process.

To Finish

When you come out of the relaxation, if you are lying down take a few moments to roll on to your side before sitting up; if you are sitting, stretch a moment before standing. Then just sit and breathe for a while, with your eyes lowered, feeling the quiet around you, appreciating your body, your mind, your environment and the world that you are about to rejoin.

The Practice

Included in this chapter are instructions for two Inner Conscious Relaxation practices that start the same but then diverge. You can read these instructions on to a tape so that you can play it back whenever you want to practise, or you can have a friend do it so that the voice is not your own. You may want to have very soft music playing in the background. Each of these practices should last for about thirty minutes. Alternatively, a number of relaxation and meditation tapes are available from the address on page 174.

Practice – Inner Conscious Relaxation No.1

General instructions
Remove any watches, belts or glasses that may restrict the flow of your energy. Find a quiet place to lie on the floor. Have a blanket or mat beneath you, a pillow under your head, and a light blanket to cover you. Your arms should be parallel to your body with your palms upward, legs slightly apart and eyes closed. If you

need to sit in a chair use a straight-backed one, and sit with both your feet flat on the ground, hands resting palm upwards on your thighs, head tilted neither up nor down. Adjust your body until you find a position you can keep throughout the practice. Take a deep breath and let it go.

During Inner Conscious Relaxation your eyes are closed but you are neither asleep nor externalised. Your awareness is in the space between sleep and wakefulness. It is important to stay awake and focused. This is not a concentration or meditation – you simply maintain an unbroken stream of awareness throughout. In this way you relax into the essence of your being, letting go of any resistance to the peace and happiness that is healing and abundant within you.

First phase
Start by relaxing your body mentally. Do this by bring-ing your awareness to your toes and working your way up through your body. Use your mind like a flashlight, releasing tension wherever it may appear. The toes ... feet ... ankles ... calves ... knees ... thighs ... buttocks ... back ... genitals ... pelvis ... stomach ... navel ... chest ... fingers ... hands ... wrists ... elbows ... upper arms ... shoulders ... neck ... head.

Now become aware of your breathing. As you follow these instructions, stay with your breath. Repeat silently to yourself, 'I am aware I am practising Inner Conscious Relaxation.' Repeat this three times. Watch the incoming and the outgoing breath, inhaling and exhaling naturally but with awareness.

Now create a resolve, a *sankalpa*. It should be a state-ment or affirmation concerning your life that is uplifting, inspiring and meaningful to you. Repeat your resolve three times silently to yourself. At the end of the practice when you hear the words 'Peace ... Peace ... Peace', again repeat this resolve to yourself three times.

Second phase

You are now ready for the next stage: rotation of consciousness through the various parts of your body. As each part of the body is mentioned, repeat it to yourself silently and try to visualise the part in your mind, moving slowly through the body. Begin: right hand thumb ... second finger ... third finger ... fourth finger ... fifth finger ... palm ... wrist ... lower arm ... elbow ... upper arm ... shoulder ... armpit ... waist ... hip ... thigh ... knee ... calf ... ankle ... heel ... sole ... ball of the right foot ... the big toe ... second ... third ... fourth ... fifth toe ... left hand thumb ... second finger ... third ... fourth ... fifth ... palm ... wrist ... lower arm ... elbow ... upper arm ... shoulder ... armpit ... waist ... hip ... thigh ... knee ... calf ... ankle ... heel ... sole ... ball of the left foot ... the big toe ... second ... third ... fourth ... fifth toe ... right shoulder blade ... left shoulder blade ... spinal cord ... the whole of the back ... the left buttock ... the right buttock ... genitals ... pelvis ... stomach ... navel ... right chest ... left chest ... centre of the chest ... neck ... chin ... upper lip ... lower lip ... both lips together ... nose ... nose tip ... right cheek ... left cheek ... right temple ... left temple ... right ear ... left ear ... right eye ... left eye ... right eyelid ... left eyelid ... right eyebrow ... left eyebrow ... centre of the eyebrows ... forehead ... top of the head ... back of the head ... whole body, whole body ... awareness of the whole body. Maintain awareness of your breathing for a few moments.

Third phase

Now we work with the pairs of opposites. Start by creating the feeling of heaviness in the physical body ... feel as if your legs are heavy ... your buttocks are heavy ... your back is heavy ... your arms are heavy ... your chest is heavy ... your head is heavy ... your whole body is feeling heavy ... feel as if your whole body is sinking into the ground and is getting heavier and heavier. Feel as if your body is so heavy you cannot even lift your arms. Visualise what it is to be heavy ... a lead weight is heavy ... stay with this feeling for a few moments.

Now create the feeling of lightness in the physical body ... what is lightness? A feather is light ... bring the feeling of lightness to the body ... to your fingers ... palms ... arms ... stomach ... chest ... back ... legs ... shoulders ... neck ... top of the head ... whole body, your whole body is light ... feel as if you are floating off the ground ... stay with this feeling for a few moments.

Now, what is the feeling of coldness? Can you create the feeling of coldness in your body? Your hands are cold ... your feet are cold ... your buttocks are cold ... your back is cold ... you can feel a chill up your spine ... your cheeks are cold ... your head is cold ... your whole body is getting colder and colder. What is cold? It is a wintry day and you are walking in the snow, it is so cold outside ... create coldness in your whole body ... stay with this feeling for a few moments.

Now, what is heat? Can you create heat in your body? Create the feeling of heat ... in the palm of your right hand ... in your left hand ... create heat in the sole of your right foot ... your left foot ... heat in your stomach ... your chest ... your lips ... your eyes ...

your head ... create heat in the whole of your body ...
it is a hot summer day and you are in the desert, the
noonday sun is above ... you feel the heat and are
sweating ... stay with this feeling for a few moments.

Fourth phase

Now you are ready for the next stage of ICR – visualisation. Become aware of your heart. Your heart is like
a beautiful flower that when open reveals a great love,
a great peace. Feel as if you are going on a journey into
the heart. The visualisations will take you deeper into
this reservoir of pure love. This is the experience of
the essence of your being.

Visualise a red rose ... see the rose, its colour and
texture ... smell its sweetness ... visualise it opening
and feel that your heart is also opening. Visualise the
small flame of a candle ... see the candle flame getting
bigger and bigger ... feel the warmth of the flame.
Visualise a mother embracing her newborn child ...
feel the unconditional love that exists between these
two. Visualise a church ... inside the church the
congregation is immersed in prayer. Visualise smoke
rising from a chimney ... inside the house a fire is
burning in the grate ... people are gathered around the
fireplace ... there is a feeling of friendship and love.
Visualise someone rowing a boat on a lake ... you can
see the ripples made by the oars and the calmness of
the water ... you can see the stillness at the bottom of
the lake. Visualise the Virgin Mary ... she is full of
mercy. Visualise children playing in a green field.
Visualise a full moon on a starlit night.

Now imagine in your heart that you are walking
along a beautiful sandy beach ... the blue sea is calm,
the sun is shining and the sky is clear. You are alone

on the beach, it is early morning ... in the distance
you see a figure coming towards you ... as you walk
towards each other you see it is a holy man, he is
smiling with a look of great tenderness and compassion
... his body is glowing ... you can feel great love
emanating from him. As he greets you, his peace
enters you like a warm friendly embrace, a feeling of
unconditional acceptance and love ... you walk along
the beach together, and as you walk you notice that he
leaves no footprints in the sand.

Peace, peace, peace. Become aware of the resolve
that you made at the beginning of the practice ...
repeat it three times to yourself.

Now become aware of your breathing, watch the
inhalation and exhalation ... continue for a few
moments ... become aware of the room you are in ...
now move your fingers and toes ... externalise your
consciousness ... keeping your eyes closed ... the
practice of ICR is over.

When you are ready slowly roll over on to your side,
then gently sit up. Spend a few moments watching
your breath. Have a smile on your face.

Practice – Inner Conscious Relaxation No.2

Follow the general instructions in Inner Conscious
Relaxation No.1, through the first and second phases.

Third phase
Become aware of the contact between your physical
body and the ground beneath you ... wherever your
body meets the ground bring your attention to that
place. Beginning with your right leg and the ground ...
just be aware of the point of contact and focus your

attention on that space ... stay with that for a few moments. Now bring your awareness to the point of contact of your left leg and the ground ... bring your awareness to that space ... stay with your awareness there for a few moments.

Now bring your awareness to the meeting point of your right arm and the ground ... awareness of that space between your arm and the ground. Now bring your awareness to the meeting point of your left arm and the ground ... focus your attention on that space. Now bring your attention to your buttocks and the ground ... awareness of the meeting point and the space ... stay with this awareness. Now bring your awareness to the point of contact between your back and the ground ... focus on the space between the two ... stay with this for a few moments.

Now bring your awareness to the meeting point between the back of your head and the ground ... now to the meeting point of the whole of your physical body and the ground ... just focus on that space where your physical body and the ground meet and get closer to the awareness of this space. This will help you let go and enter into a deeper sense of relaxation and ease.

Now become aware of heart-centred breathing. When we bring the breath into the heart we release the tension in this area and awaken the love within. Simply focus awareness in the centre of your chest – the heartspace – and watch as you breathe in and out ... count the breaths, starting at one and going up to ten, one number with each breath. When you reach ten begin to count down to one. If you lose the count, just start at one again. Feel as if you are sinking into your heart and entering a vast ocean of love. Your breath is like a raft carrying you on this ocean.

Fourth phase

Now visualise yourself in a far-off tropical island. There are animals living there: lion, tiger, cobra, elephant, monkey and deer ... they are living in peace together. Visualise yourself walking into a beautiful forest with trees and flowers all around you ... the air is pure, fresh with the sweet scent of the flowers ... you feel alive and part of nature ... birds are singing ... it feels familiar ... you feel at home.

Then you see in the distance a fire burning ... you feel drawn to this fire ... you notice people sitting in a circle around the fire making offerings of herbs and sacred ash ... a holy woman is sitting with them and is chanting 'Om'. There is a great feeling of joy in your heart ... a sense of happiness is awakened by this sight. You are invited to join the circle ... as you come closer you notice that the people in the circle are your friends ... people you have always known. The holy woman appears like a goddess ... radiant ... luminous ... compassionate ... as you sit together there is a great feeling of oneness ... a realisation that you are loved totally and completely and that all beings and creatures are your friends ... that in essence there is no separation, only the one pure light that illuminates all hearts. The realisation of unconditional happiness fills your heart.

Peace, peace, peace. Become aware of the resolve that you made at the beginning of the practice ... repeat it three times to yourself.

Now become aware of your breathing, watch the inhalation and exhalation ... continue for a few moments ... become aware of the room you are in ... now move your fingers and toes ... externalise your consciousness ... keeping your eyes closed ... the practice of ICR is over.

When you are ready slowly roll over on your side, then gently sit up. Have a smile on your face.

Chapter 7

All in the Mind's Eye

The power of the mind is so great that it goes beyond our imagination. We can use that power to create either destructive and harmful forces or we can use it to create constructive and healing energies. In relaxation we use the mind to enter an alpha state in order to let go of any stress or tension and generate a refreshed and replenished state; in meditation we focus the mind on one thing – such as the breath – to find the space between the thoughts, a place of profound peace. With creative visualisation we use the relaxation principle of entering deeply into ourselves and then bring the power of the mind to create healing and uplifting images for specific purposes.

To show you the power of visualisation, close your eyes and, just for a few moments, imagine a gruesome scene from a horror movie; then feel how the muscles in your back, shoulders or stomach contract. Or imagine yourself having a cold shower and feel the goosebumps appearing. Or see yourself doing some aerobic exercise and feel your muscles contract and expand with the imagined movement. Now visualise yourself walking on a sandy beach, the sun is hot and the sea is lapping at your feet; watch your body open and relax. All you are doing is thinking different images, but the body is immediately responding.

We can use creative visualisation to generate physical healing; to strengthen and invigorate our health; to develop an inner calm; to access parts of our being with which we feel out of touch; or to develop aspects of our being that we feel we are lacking. Many spiritual practices use visualisation for creating different states of mind. Tibetan Buddhism, for instance, is full of deeply intricate visualisations aimed at loosening the hold of the ego and awakening certain conditions of mind. Visualisation is a way of communicating with the unconscious and of altering long-established behaviour patterns. It is not a way of pretending that we are different from how we are, or of generating false hope, but a way of opening our mind to our innermost potential.

Visualisation shows us that all the knowledge and insight we need is already within us: we could not create something that we do not already have. Neither the images that arise nor any words of guidance we may receive are from some outside place or person. All we are doing is tapping into the source of wisdom that is always there and making it more accessible by bringing it to the conscious mind. For instance, during a workshop Debbie led a guided visualisation to meet with a wise being. One of the participants, James, met an old crone by a fire and was given some advice that was particularly important for him at that time – it helped move him through a state of feeling stuck and dull. Afterwards, as we talked about it, Debbie gently pointed out that this advice had come from within him, and that it had been there all along. It touched James very deeply to realise that he already had the answers he was seeking, and even more so that it had come from the feminine part of his being. Visualisation uses the language of the unconscious – that of imagery and the senses – in order to unlock the wisdom we already have.

A few people find visualisation difficult – images do not appear to them. However, most of us have at least one sense faculty that can lead us into deeper states of awareness, whether it is touch, sight, sound or smell. When doing any visualisation it is important to try to include all the senses; doing so makes the image more deeply embodied and our physical body will get the message. We also need to include the emotions, which is why it is so important to use images that feel good, have meaning and resonate with our feelings. If we use images that we do not believe in, the visualisation will be of little use. We can also look at pictures in order to stimulate the images inside us.

Healing Visualisation

The use of specific visualisation images has been helpful with many illnesses, the best documented being cancer. The idea is to create an image that brings healing through either calming or energising the body. It is essential to find an image that works for you and feels appropriate to the healing that is needed. It helps to try to *feel* what your body needs – whether it wants to calm or cool down or to become more vibrant – and to feel the needs of each particular area. For instance, you might want to visualise cool yogurt being rubbed into hot and swollen joints; warmth pouring into cold or paralysed limbs, perhaps in the form of gold or deep red light; or an overworked brain might benefit from an image of waves gently lapping a soft, sandy shoreline.

Because of the perverse laws of nature, when we reject something it comes running after us, and when we go after something it keeps eluding us. In the same way, if you try to combat a malady, or to wipe it out by rejecting it, the chances are it will just reappear elsewhere. When finding an image for your own healing use one that embraces rather than rejects your body. Meeting physical pain with a mentally aggressive or hateful attitude brings more pain into the body. Making friends with your pain by offering a soothing, loving and compassionate image will help bring a deeper level of healing.

This has been seen in the various images used with cancer, which range from video game images that gobble up their enemy through knights on white horses lancing the cancer cells, to seeing the cancer as a lost part of us that needs to be loved, or the cells as containing unexpressed love which, as they are embraced, is released to nourish the body. Images that focus on the immune cells becoming stronger and more effective range from seeing them as rabbits breeding rapidly, through ministers, angels or mother figures dressed in white, to garbage disposal men sweeping up the rubbish!

You can visualise parts of your body working again that are not functioning well at present, such as the circulation or nervous system. If it is difficult to visualise them in their physical form, find an image that represents these parts. For instance, visualise steel or plastic pipes for veins, a telephone exchange system or electricity wires for the nervous system. The most important thing is to find an image that speaks to you.

Practice – Hot Hands

This technique teaches you how to use the power of your mind. Try using different heat-creating images to bring warmth to cold hands or cold feet. Find a comfortable place to sit where you will be undisturbed for a few minutes. Close your eyes, take a deep breath and let it go. Spend a few moments just watching the flow of your breath as it enters and leaves, feeling yourself relaxing and getting quieter with each breath.

Now begin to focus on your right hand, or whichever part you want to get warm. Do nothing and think nothing – just put all your energy into this area. And imagine that hand getting hotter and hotter. It may help to imagine the sun beating down on your hand, or to imagine that you are holding red-hot coals. Focus all your attention on feeling this hand getting hotter and hotter. You may even find that it begins to perspire. Keep doing this for at least four or five minutes.

If you need to, visualise your hand cooling down a little before you move on. Now direct your attention to any other part of your body that needs warming and repeat the process. When you are ready to finish, take a deep breath and gently open your eyes.

If images do not come readily to meet your physical requirement, let your body tell you what it needs. Do this by spending a few moments relaxing and then visualise the part of your body that is in need, or bring your attention to focus on that part. Just breathe into this part, getting to know it, feeling at ease with it, breathing into any tension or pain. Then gently ask it what it is trying to tell you, what its needs are and how you can help. Open yourself to communicating in this way with your body so that it may speak to you. Often spontaneous images will appear that tell you a great deal about the bodymind implications of the difficulty. More information and instruction on this point are contained in Debbie's book *Your Body Speaks Your Mind* and a tape is available from the authors (see p. 174).

A different healing visualisation involves imagining your-self in a beautiful place that you feel is particularly healing – perhaps a temple or sacred building or somewhere in nature. If you can create this place, spend some time exploring it. Then imagine there is someone else there – perhaps a wise old woman, a healing figure of some kind, perhaps an angel or special doctor. Let the image arise spontaneously in your visualisation. You meet this person and they bring healing to your body, whether through touching you, or through giving you special herbs to drink, or through their words. Absorb the healing they offer you. Take it into the core of your being.

If visualisation is hard for you, try listening to different sounds to generate healing. Try running water, birdsong or gentle music, for example. Each sound has a different effect – find the one that generates the greatest sense of calm and ease within you. Or explore different smells through aromatherapy oils, as each one is associated with a different aspect of healing. Find the one that you resonate with most deeply and use it in your relaxation. The more you can listen to your own body and respond to its needs, the deeper your experience of inner healing.

It is important, as with any practice, to maintain your visualisation regularly, so as to build up a strong foundation of concentration and communication. Don't just do it once and then wonder why it is not working! To practise, enter into a deeply relaxed state as described in Chapter 6. Then bring into your mind the image that works for you. Keep to the same image for as long as it feels right. Stay with it, feeling it in the relevant part of your body, for at least ten to fifteen minutes. Repeat this twice a day if possible.

Stress Release Visualisation

To enhance stress release and inner relaxation you need to create images into which you can completely let go without effort, complications or resistance. They should be images that embrace you and make you feel loved and soothed, images that you can sink into. When you do this, first the stress in the body eases and then the stress in the mind begins to be released.

For instance, visualise yourself walking along a beautiful beach, feeling the sun on your face, the sand between your toes, the water lapping gently. Then visualise yourself floating in the water, which is warm and makes your body gently sway. As you lie there all the tension in your body is released, and you feel completely soft and loved. Hear the waves breaking on the shore and the birds singing, taste the refreshing coolness, your breath flowing with the rhythm of the gentle waves.

Alternatively, visualise yourself walking down a country lane in the summer afternoon sun, listening to the birds singing, smelling the sweet air – bring all your senses into the visualisation. Then you come to a gate, and when you go through it you enter the most beautiful garden with luxuriant flowers, shady trees and a soft lawn. Bees are humming, birds darting at the edge of a wild pond, a few swans swim past and the air is laden with summer scents. You are completely at ease here; you are safe, relaxed and feel great happiness.

These images will give you ideas for creating your own. Try visualising a secret place that was always just for you, somewhere private and special where you were very happy. Imagine all the details of this place so that you feel as if you are there. Or create a new place, somewhere that feels very safe and is completely separate from the rest of your life – no familiar landmarks, no familiar faces, places or situations. Explore the elements that are there – the air, temperature, ground, colours, sounds and smells. This place is just for you; it is your private space where you can truly be at ease, where you can let go of everything in your daily life and just be with yourself. Or try creating a special place such as a sanctuary or temple within you. Visualise the beauty of this sanctuary – perhaps glowing stained-glass windows or rich tapestries on the walls, ancient stone floors or thickly carpeted rooms, well-worn wooden pews or soft embroidered cushions. Create the most perfect sacred space and feel yourself to be in that space, perhaps in prayer or meditation.

You may find you meet people in your visualisation, such as a wise old man or a beautiful gentle woman, a small friendly being or even an animal. These represent aspects of your own self; they are there to help you, befriend you, and guide you deeper to your happiness and peace. Listen to discover if they have anything to say to you, receive anything they may have to give you. Each time you go to your special place it will be different, so be aware of the differences and what they are teaching you.

Another stress-releasing visualisation involves focusing on a particular area of stress in your life and seeing it as healed, whole, completely stress-free. This means dropping your present images or feelings about this part of your life and allowing yourself to open to a whole new way of seeing things. This is possible when we remember that nothing is permanent, that all things pass. Remembering this enables us to imagine a situation different from how it is at present – imagine it full of compassion, love, healing, respect and acceptance. Let yourself sink into this image, purposely creating the opposite image of however you normally perceive it. And let events unfold. New insight may emerge on how to deal with your situation, or changes may happen without you having to actually do anything. The power of the mind is, after all, unlimited.

Practice – Trading Places with the Buddha

One way to help you go beyond your limitations or conflicts is to re-create scenes in your mind but with a different player. Imagine a situation you are trying to resolve: a problem in your life, or an area of stress and conflict. Re-create all the details in your mind but, instead of yourself, visualise either a meaningful religious or spiritual teacher or someone whom you consider really wise, such as the Buddha or Jesus standing in your place.

Watch what happens. How do they deal with the situation? How different is it from the way you deal with it? What effect do they have on the other people in your visualisation? What can you learn from this? Remember, whatever wisdom or compassion this person comes up with in your visualisation has actually come from your own imagination: it is already within you.

Self-renewal Visualisation

We can use visualisation to connect with qualities or aspects of ourselves that we feel we are either out of touch with or that we would like more of in our lives. Forgiveness, inner peace, patience, compassion and intuitive insight are some typical examples.

In this context the visualisation becomes more of an inner journey. As the journey unfolds, step by step, it takes you deeper into yourself, through layers of tension, through the conscious mind and into the unconscious. Eventually you will arrive at a special place where you meet either a figure such as a guide or teacher, or an animal, or an object like a flower or a crystal – something that represents this particular quality you want to have more of in your life. Having met your figure, animal or object, you can share anything you want to with them, and listen to see if they have anything they wish to say to you. You may want to take a gift for them; and you may be given a special object or gift, symbolising this quality, that you can take into your heart and gain strength from at any time. There is a visualisation for this on p.105. You can follow it, or learn from it how to create your own journey, alternatively visualisation tapes are available from the address on p.174.

When we open ourselves to exploring our inner world in this way many different images, colours or symbols can arise, all with meaning or lessons for us. For instance, Debbie led a visualisation with a group where she guided them through an image of the countryside until they came to an old wood. 'At the entrance to the wood there is a path leading into a clearing, to a glade where the sun is shining on a figure waiting to greet you,' she said. 'However, as you begin along the path there are a few small obstacles that have to be overcome in order for you to get to the glade.'

Afterwards, we asked the participants what obstacles they had encountered. One person had to climb over fallen logs, another had to cut his way through a thick bramble bush, while yet another found that the path had disappeared and she had to look quite hard under stones and moss to find it again. What was fascinating was how appropriate the images were to their lives. Each of the obstacles described fitted the difficulties that that person was dealing with, while also giving them greater insight into how to overcome them. For the obstacles and the insight, as well as the wise figure or guiding angel that represents the quality we would like more of, and the quality itself, are all already within us.

The images you obtain in your own visualisation may not be immediately understandable – the language of the unconscious can be dream-like and symbolic rather than factual. It is helpful to write down any images that come to you and keep them in your mind for a few days, or until the meaning becomes clearer. The same image can mean something very different to each person. Trust your own instinctive response to the image, bring it into your meditation and ask for more information, or simply let it speak to you in its own time.

How to Do It

You can do short visualisations anywhere – in the office, the toilet, your bedroom, even in the back of a taxi! Just don't do it while you are driving or operating machinery. And you can do longer visualisations when you have the time and know you will not be disturbed. You can lie down or sit in an upright chair. You might want a light blanket to keep you warm, and you may like to play some soft music. Loosen any belts or restrictive clothing, glasses and watches.

Before starting any visualisation, always take a few minutes to quieten your mind and body. Read the instructions at the beginning of the practice described below. When you feel completely at ease and relaxed, repeat silently to yourself, 'My body is relaxed. My heartbeat is normal. My mind is calm and peaceful. My heart is open and loving.' Repeat this three times. Then begin your visualisation – whether it be imagining healing in your body or going on an inner journey. Stay with the visualisation as long as it feels comfortable – perhaps twenty or thirty minutes.

When you feel ready to end the imagery, take a few

moments to gently connect with and feel your body, to focus on your breathing, and to become aware of the ground you are lying on or the chair you are sitting on. Do not jump up as soon as the session is over – you have to make the transition back into your normal waking level of consciousness. Have a good stretch and open your eyes, but stay still for a few moments and just be aware of the room around you before you slowly move.

Practice – Journey to Your Inner Truth

(20–30 minutes)

Start by finding a comfortable place to sit or lie down and make sure you will not be disturbed. If you are sitting, use a straight-backed chair and place both feet flat on the floor (not crossed) and your hands on your thighs, palms upwards. If you are lying down, place your feet slightly apart and your arms by your sides, palms upwards. You may want a light blanket to cover you, and a small pillow under your head. Close your eyes.

Begin by relaxing your body. Starting at the feet, tighten the muscles, hold, then completely let go and relax your feet. Now your calf muscles: tightening, holding and releasing. Now the thighs: tighten, hold and release. Both legs are relaxed and at ease. Breathe into your legs and feel them letting go. Now go to your buttocks: tensing, holding and releasing. Work your way up the whole of your back: tensing, holding and letting go. Then the lower abdomen … the midriff … the chest. Then move to your hands … the lower arms and upper arms … then the shoulders: tensing, holding and releasing. Both arms and shoulders are completely relaxed and letting go. Now your neck ... relax all the muscles in your face ... and then the whole of your head. Feel your whole body relaxing, letting go, sinking into the ground.

Now become aware of the movement of your breath as it enters and leaves your body. Begin to feel yourself letting go as you breathe – breathing out tension on the out breath, breathing in relaxation on the in breath. As you watch the breath begin silently to count one number at the end of each out breath. Start at ten, and continue down to zero. With each breath feel your body becoming heavy and relaxing. Your mind is releasing, becoming quieter. Repeat silently to yourself, 'My body is released and relaxed. My heart-beat is normal. My mind is calm and peaceful. My heart is open and loving.' Repeat this three times.

Now begin to imagine that each breath is actually the waves on a lake breaking softly on the shore. Imagine you are walking along a beautiful lakeside, the sun warming you, the water a clear azure blue. All around you are mountains and tall trees, birds swooping in the sky. You are alone here but you feel wonderfully safe, as if being held in the palm of a hand. It is so warm and safe that you take off your clothes and lie on the shore close to the water. And the waves and your breath merge. As you breathe in you feel the wave break gently over your body. As you breathe out the wave recedes, taking with it any tension you may be feeling. Stay with this for a few moments.

Then you rise and enter the water, your body able to swim and play as the cleansing and refreshing qualities of the water revitalise your whole being. You laugh at the beauty of the sun catching the splashes, at the purity of the water, at the feeling of being loved and caressed. You float and merge with the gentle rhythm of the lake. Stay with this for a few minutes.

Then, as you swim further into the lake, you notice a cascading waterfall on the other side, falling over rocks and ferns and creating deep pools. You swim to the waterfall and play there, standing beneath the cascading water or diving into pools, like a child, carefree and timeless. Hear the water splashing, smell the freshness.

After a while you notice beyond the waterfall a cave; a gentle light seems to be glowing from it. The closer you get, the stronger the light becomes. The sweet smell of rose or sandalwood is in the air. As you enter the cave you see in the centre a large crystal, glowing with pure white light. It seems to welcome you in, as if you are expected. Then you see facing the crystal an old woman, sitting quietly, white hair falling down her back, a look of profound peace on her face. Silently you sit beside her, the light illuminating you, and a warmth comes from the woman that warms your body.

After a few moments she speaks to you. She has words of healing for you. In response you speak to her, sharing your heart, your troubles or your dreams. She gives you guidance and words of wisdom. As you look at her you feel a depth of love you have never known before. Then she hands you a gift, something special which represents that love. You hold it to your chest and it dissolves into your heart. It will always be there for you to draw strength from.

Stay a few moments more before you rise, then make your way out of the cave and on to the bank above the lake. There you find a set of new clothes waiting for you, the softest of clothes that feel like silk and are the palest of colours. As you walk back along the edge of the lake you pass your old clothes, discarded on the shore. You do not need them any more. There is a relief in letting them go. Gently you walk back into your normal life.

Let the visualisation fade. Take a deep breath and become aware of your body on the floor or in the chair. Spend a few moments breathing and reconnecting. Then stretch your legs and arms. When you feel ready, very gently open your eyes and greet your world.

PART THREE

AWAKENING THE SLEEPING BUDDHA

Chapter 8

The Journey
Is the Goal

In this third part of the book we explore the many facets of meditation, looking first at meditation as a whole and at some of its effects, and then at how to practise. In the final chapter we offer a number of meditation techniques with full instructions.

Concentrating on a Single Form

The basis of all meditation is concentration. The Buddha explained that the mind is like the flame on a log – it needs something to burn. In order to reach a quiet space within ourselves we need to give the mind something to occupy it, so that its normal myriad concerns can be focused on something other than themselves. By giving the mind a form on which to concentrate it slowly becomes more one-pointed, focused and quiet.

In a way it does not matter what the form is, it could be

anything that we feel akin to. But traditionally there are specific objects and there is a reason for this – they are the most conducive to developing a concentrated or one-pointed state. As Jessica McBeth points out in *Moon Over Water*. 'The word concentrate is derived from words meaning to join in one centre.' The practice or technique is there to gather us in, to unite our energies, to focus us in one place. Meditation is simply being with that object or form and letting attentiveness fill our whole being.

The best-known objects are the breath, a repeated sound or mantra, a candle, or even the thoughts themselves. There are numerous forms of meditation built up around one or more of these objects, and most of us will find that we resonate with one particular form more than another. However, no one technique is better than any other. Through concentrating on our chosen object, by paying attention to it, becoming one with it, sitting quietly and steadily with it, we dissolve the endless thought patterns and enter into a more profound spaciousness.

It is advisable to try any one form of meditation for at least three months. By doing a particular form consistently we experience greater benefits. Repetition is vital to stop the mind being pulled into different directions, for it to go beyond doubt and confusion, boredom and lethargy, and for us to go deeper into ourselves. As meditation becomes more familiar we become less concerned with technique. The practice is just a raft – a means of getting from one shore to the other – and any technique that enables us to enter a still and aware place will achieve this. There are many types of raft and many places to cross the river, and the aim of them all is to end up on the other side. Once there we no longer need the raft: there is nowhere to move on to, simply a process of becoming more and more present.

There is no one way to practise – there are as many ways

as there are people, as many techniques as there are teachers. Trust your own judgement – what is important is that the practice works for you. Here is a delightful story that illustrates how all ways are valid and how the attitude of the practitioner is more important than the technique.

A monk had been meditating in a cave for many, many years. All this time he had been alone, absorbed in his meditation, slowly dissolving all distractions until he abided only in pure mind. His practice was the recitation of a mantra, and each day he would repeat the words of his mantra over and over again.

The cave he lived in was on the edge of a great lake. One day another monk was passing in a boat when he heard the sound of the mantra being intoned coming from the cave. He was concerned and immediately rowed to the shore to talk with the monk. 'Brother,' he said, 'you have been practising for so long, for so many years, but you have got the mantra wrong! Now let me show you, for if you do the right mantra you will soon develop great insights and extraordinary powers. You will be able to walk on water and do whatever you want!'

'Oh dear,' said the first monk. 'After all that! You had better tell me the proper mantra now and I will start to practise it immediately.' So the visiting monk told him the proper pronunciation of the mantra and went on his way.

However, he had not been back on the lake rowing his boat for long when he heard a shout from the shore. The first monk was standing there waving to him. 'Wait!' he called. Then he picked up the hem of his robe and quickly walked across the water to the waiting boat. 'Brother,' he said to the visiting monk. 'I've forgotten the proper mantra. What was it again?'

Training the Mind

As explained above, all forms of meditation are aimed at focusing our minds, which are normally far from quiet. There is an incessant dialogue of thoughts and feelings, scenarios and dramas, fears and anxieties, dreams and longings all demanding to be heard. And not only is there a constant stream of noise in our heads, but we rarely allow time to let that noise settle. Our thoughts and impulses often seem to 'run through the mind like a coursing river', as Jon Kabat-Zinn says in *Mindfulness Meditation*. 'We get caught up in the torrent and it winds up submerging our lives .... Meditation means learning how to let go of this current, sit by its bank and listen to it; learn from it, and then use its energies to guide us rather than tyrannise us.'

As we practise, the more scattered and distracted aspects begin to settle and we start to see the contents of our minds more objectively. This may take a while, for we have a life-time of mental habits and patterns to let go of. But as we continue opening further we connect with a quiet stillness beneath all the chatter, a vast and uncontainable spacious-ness. We may only dip in and out of this spaciousness, tasting it for just a moment, or perhaps a few moments between thoughts, but it is always there. Meditation occurs in that space between the thoughts. It does not matter if we practise just five minutes a day, or for an hour a day, or if we participate in a long retreat. What matters is that we are opening to ourselves – we are creating a space in which we can explore the wonders of our own being and discover a deeper level of happiness. Throughout the ages and through-out all spiritual traditions, meditation has been the tool used for accessing this deep inner place of peace and wisdom.

Meditation has very physical benefits, many of which are a continuation from the benefits of deep relaxation. As we practise, blood pressure lowers and tension and stress-related difficulties reduce, the nervous system is calmed throughout the body, and metabolism and oxygen intake slow down. Depression, fear and anxiety are lifted. By paying attention to the object of our meditation, we become aware of the inner dialogue – the feelings, thoughts and scenarios that arise in our minds. As these diminish, we expand our awareness to levels of pain or suffering that may lie beneath them. If we are able just to be with this, softly embracing ourselves as we are, without judgement or resistance, they are healed. Their place is taken by a growing optimism, creativity and sense of self – we feel more in touch with ourselves, our feelings, our place in the world. And as we continue, something more enduring and powerful emerges that embraces and nourishes us – a sense of coming home.

As with any activity, it can take time to feel the benefits. Yet how anxious we are to see results, to feel that something is happening! It can take five years to train as a doctor, even three years to learn flower arranging, and learning how to train our minds is a lot harder than that. Remember, your mind has been a free agent for maybe thirty, forty or fifty years, and now you are trying to bring it to one place, to focus it on one thing. Be patient, and within a few weeks you will notice changes. These may not be in the practice itself but in the rest of your life, such as in your attitudes, tolerance level and happiness.

Practice – Just Breathing

Find a comfortable place to sit. Close your eyes and feel your body relaxing. Spend a few moments appreciating yourself, your seat and the world around you.

Now bring your attention to your breath. Where do you most feel the breath? Follow the movement of the breath from where it enters at the tip of the nose all the way to the belly, and see where your attention is most keen. Feel the breath entering and leaving. What sensations are there? Does it feel hot or cool? Is it short or quick? Is there a pause between breaths or between the inhalation and exhalation? Just watch the breath, observe its natural movement, be aware that you are breathing. Closely observe every detail about the breath from the place where your attention rests – the tip of the nose, chest or belly. Watch one whole breath entering and filling and leaving and emptying, then watch another, and then another.

Do this for a few moments or for as long as you like whenever you like. When you are ready, gently become aware of your body and of the room around you, and take a deep, grateful breath.

Ordinary Magic

When you practise meditation you may find a curious change taking place in the rest of your life. It is a sense of something out of the ordinary, yet which at the same time feels absolutely ordinary and as it should be – a sort of magical quality, a growing sense of wonder and beauty, an appreciation of the subtler levels of life, of a flow or pulse that reaches beyond your individual self.

Magic is usually regarded as something extra-ordinary – something that takes us out of our normal perception of reality. While our ordinary world appears limited and confined, magic makes us aware of a different reality some-where beyond its boundaries. It is exciting because of the very irrationality that it embodies – it takes us through our limited conceptions and beliefs and cannot be understood with the rational mind. Meditation has a similar effect: it takes us beyond our normal mind, through boundaries or limitations, and opens us to new ways of seeing and being.

'One of the most profound experiences I have had during meditation occurred after a few months. I felt a shaft of light flow through my body, the light flowed deeply inside me from the top of my head down to the ground. I felt a tremendous peace and connection to the life force. Afterwards everything appeared vibrant and very colourful and rich. I felt a great joy in simply being alive.'

Divya

The world around us appears to possess a luminosity that we were unaware of before. There is magic in the fact that we breathe, that we can taste, touch and smell, that our heart is beating. There is magic in the sun shining, the rain falling, the plants growing. There is magic in our feet on the earth, in the wind on our faces, in a beautiful sunset, in a bird soaring. This is the beauty of ordinary things that permeates our world, but that we rarely appreciate unless we go beyond the rational and logical mind.

In the simplicity and stillness of meditation arises an awareness of these subtler and more illusory qualities. The magic is all around us, in everything, unassuming, un-demanding, just being ordinary. It is the worry, confusions and anxieties that are extra-ordinary. When we let go of the 'extra', we sink into the 'ordinary' beauty of things as they are. This is seen in a Japanese haiku poem that reads:

Among the grasses
An unknown flower
Blooming white.

It is as if we have moved from a place of not noticing the trees or the birds in the sky, through awakening an awareness that fills our world with meaning and vibrancy, to seeing all things just as they are – a part of the whole, an expression of reality, emptiness in form, form in emptiness. In the same way, we move from a place of having little awareness or knowledge of ourselves to uncovering a world within filled with both the beautiful and the not so beautiful; and from there to a place of embracing ourselves just as we are, and in doing that to finding we are a part of a much bigger picture. We move from a deficient sense of ourselves to discovering our strength and confidence, and from there to unconditional happiness. 'If we open our eyes, if we open our minds, if we open our hearts, we will find that this world is a magical place,' wrote Chögyam Trungpa in *Shambhala*. 'However, the discovery of that magic can happen only when we transcend the embarrassment about being alive, when we have the bravery to proclaim the goodness and dignity of human life, without either hesitation or arrogance.'

On Having No Reason

But all the above are not reasons for practising meditation! In fact, we want to leave all reasons behind. We practise meditation simply because it feels right and we enjoy the way we feel. If there is any other motivation, we will surely be thwarted. For meditation is an experience of being. It does not lead us anywhere, we do not have a goal that we are trying to reach; the experience itself is the purpose. Through the experience of just being with ourselves – of just sitting and breathing, watching thoughts, becoming quiet – change will come naturally. That is why meditation is often referred to as a path: the journey itself is the goal.

If we have a purpose to our practice, such as achieving a quiet mind or discovering magic, we will start trying to achieve it and immediately we will no longer just be paying attention. We will be trying. The trying creates a distraction, followed by more tension, and we get further and further away from a quiet mind. When we want to achieve something, the wanting or trying is using up the space in which it can happen.

'When I began to meditate my reactions were ones of scepticism – I really could not figure out what was going on or what I was meant to be doing. I didn't understand that the whole purpose was just to "be" and not to "do" anything – so I just sat there getting bored!'

Sonya

Each time you sit and practise it will be different – this is normal. Periods of complete quiet or inner spaciousness may be very short. The progress you make occurs as you are able to bring your mind to a quiet place more readily. And although the mind might learn to stay quiet, that does not mean that discursive thoughts or unconscious memories will not suddenly surface and bring with them all sorts of images and feelings. Meditation is a space in which you are alert, focused and aware. It is not a trance-like state, you are not sitting there doing nothing, nor are you being selfish or self-absorbed. It is not strenuous or rigorous; it is about stopping and being still. Nothing else – just being still. You are watching the mind, sitting with whatever arises in it without judgement or criticism, simply observing, being quiet and getting in touch with the you beneath the thoughts.

In that stillness you meet yourself, find yourself and become friends with yourself. It means being totally present, here, now. As soon as you drift off somewhere you are no longer present and no longer being still. All you have to do is focus on your object of concentration. If your mind wanders, gently bring it back to your object. There should be no tension in trying to hold on to your concentration, for that would be defeating the purpose of the exercise. You are simply embracing yourself in a peaceful and tender space, within which you focus your mind.

Experiences on the Journey

When we first begin meditating, it can either feel absolutely wonderful, peaceful, full of visions and insights, as if we have finally come home; or it can be boring, difficult to focus, uncomfortable if not painful, and seeming only to create more tension. We may have a blissful and peaceful session one day, only to be followed by a session the next day in which we do nothing but think about what to cook for dinner or what to say at an imminent business meeting. We may suddenly be beset with negative feelings, strong desires bubbling up to tell someone how much we resent them or wish they would change, or we may be overcome by feelings of warmth, tenderness and compassion. We may want to laugh or cry or shout. As we relax more, so feelings that have been locked into the mind and body for a long time are free to be released and healed. Many different feelings, memories or images may arise. Just breathe into them, keep your body relaxed and let the emotions pass through you. Observe them without getting attached or drawn into them. You may have only a fraction of quiet within a whole half hour of sitting.

There is no straight path on which we start with a confused and chattering mind and end with a perfectly calm and serene mind, never to experience distracting thoughts again. But after a while the extremes do balance out: our practice may not be so ecstatic, but neither is it too repetitious. This is where we need to develop a greater level of application and concentration so that our experience goes deeper.

> '*For a long while I experienced nothing at all in meditation, but one day a huge rush of emotion surfaced from nowhere, suddenly tears were welling up followed by an enormous sense of relief.*'
>
> Sonya

> '*I began to feel a tight pain around my heart as I meditated. The harder I tried to breathe into my chest, the more suffocating the pain became. With advice and support I continued to meditate, even though I thought that if my heart did open it would be so painful that I wouldn't be able to bear it. Then one day, while meditating with a group of caring and loving people, I simply let go. And inside my heart was a beautiful garden of pure unconditional love, for myself and for those around me. I had spent my career as a midwife caring for others but without this depth of compassion and love – in the last few years I had felt so dried up I had little left to give. But suddenly I had a great source of love within me and the realisation that my life was like a miracle, a very precious jewel. There was no pain in opening, only love.*'
>
> Juliette

Different physical experiences or energy changes may occur during meditation, such as feeling as if your body is a different shape or texture, or there may be a sudden wave of energy through the body that causes a jerk or muscular reaction, or perhaps the body starts to vibrate. This is the releasing of pockets of blocked energy, an opening and rebalancing. It will pass. Experiences of light, colour or sound may also occur, such as having beautiful orchestral music fill your mind, or a vision of brilliant white or iridescent coloured light. It is natural to think that these are signs that you are progressing well, although ego-endorsement is not the purpose of meditation. The only difficulty lies in our attachment to such experiences and the expectation or longing for them to happen again, followed by disappointment when they do not. This creates a distraction from our practice.

There are numerous teachings in all the meditation traditions that warn against getting distracted by such phenomena. For instance, there is the story of a Buddhist monk who had been practising very hard for many years, trying and trying to make his meditation perfect. One day he had the most wonderful vision of a beautiful golden Buddha that filled his mind with bliss. He went to see his teacher, convinced that he had attained some profound level of advancement. He explained what an extraordinary experience he had just had, describing the depth and beauty of his vision. 'Very good,' his teacher replied. 'And if you keep practising, then we may hope it will soon go away!'

The object of meditation is not to develop psychic powers or have out-of-body experiences as much as to calm the mind, to develop compassion, greater awareness and insight, to have in-the-body experiences. We are here to go beyond the ego, not to reinforce it. A student once asked Eddie if he had ever experienced another dimension. Eddie replied, 'Have you ever experienced this one?'

Travelling Alone or Together

Each one of us differs in our needs. For some, meditating alone is preferable, while others prefer to meditate with a group. When practising with others there is a sense of support, an energy that connects the group and a developing comradeship. This can be very important, especially in the early days. Many people achieve a balance by meditating alone daily and with a group once a week. If there is no local group to which you feel drawn you can always start your own, perhaps with a few interested friends. Following a meditation tape together is a good idea as it gives structured guidance.

It is always helpful to have a teacher who can guide you through the many questions, doubts, conflicts and experiences that arise. However, it is equally important to recognise the teacher within yourself. Ramana Maharshi explained that the external teacher is there to push you in from the outside so that you can experience the teacher within – in others words, to grow to trust your own judgements, intuition and insight. We all have a sleeping Buddha within us.

When looking for a teacher it is important to trust your response to this person. You may be with someone you have been told is a great teacher, but inside yourself you do not feel comfortable, or do not resonate with what he or she is saying. A good teacher should make you feel good. You need to be at ease with this person or you will not be receptive to what they are teaching. Are they teaching what you are looking for? This is a very personal experience.

Most important of all, you should feel that the teacher has heart: you are looking for someone who is warm, caring and compassionate, not arrogant, disdainful or distant. When the Vietnamese meditation teacher, Thich Nhat Hanh, was asked by one of his students if he was ready to teach, Thich Nhat Hanh replied by simply asking, 'Are you happy?' In this single question he pointed to one of the essential qualities required in a teacher, that he or she be happy within themselves.

> '*I remember meeting my first real teacher. He emanated all the qualities I wanted to have for myself. He radiated peace, joy, a great sense of humour and tremendous kindness. But what I remember most is his humility and happiness.*'
>
> Eddie

Watch your own bodily reactions, consider how you feel as you walk away, watch what you feel like a few days later. Are you being asked to believe in something or even someone that you don't want to? Are feelings coming up in you that confirm your innate beauty or reinforce your fear? Are you being asked for money or membership fees? There is nothing wrong with earning money from being a teacher, but it should certainly not be the focus of the experience. Look around you at other people who are there – talk to them, find out how they feel and see how you feel with them. Remember, a good teacher does not say that only he or she has the truth, rather they enable you to find the truth within yourself.

Explore the various traditions and teachings available and then settle with one. It is vital to give yourself time with a teacher or teaching so as to gain the greatest benefits. 'Stop shopping around and settle down and go deeply into one body of truth,' was Chögyam Trungpa's main advice. Too much diversity creates distraction and stops us going deeper into ourselves. But this does not mean that you have to stay with the same teacher for ever. We all change and have different needs at different times – no one teacher will necessarily fill all those needs.

Is Meditation Difficult or Easy?

There are few guidelines for meditation, as each one of us needs to discover what works for us, not what works for someone else. Most important of all is that meditation should not become this big 'thing' that has to be practised, regardless of everything else: let it be a naturally integrated part of your life. It should feel like a friend – something you want to be with because you enjoy it. Meditation is the development of a relationship between you and your inner self that goes on to benefit all others, not a begrudging duty that you feel you have to do. The following story illustrates these points.

There was once a famous Buddhist layman named Busol. He was deeply enlightened, as were his wife, his son and his daughter. A man came to visit him one day and asked him, 'Is meditation difficult or not?'

Busol replied, 'Oh, it is very difficult – it is like taking a stick and trying to hit the moon!'

The man was puzzled and thought, 'If meditation is so difficult, how did Busol's wife gain enlightenment?' So he went and asked her the same question.

'Meditation is the easiest thing in the world,' she replied. 'It's just like touching your nose when you wash your face in the morning!'

By now the man was thoroughly confused. 'I don't understand. Is meditation difficult or is it easy? Who is right?' he asked their son.

'Meditation is not difficult and not easy,' came the reply. 'On the tips of a hundred blades of grass is the Buddha's meaning.'

'Not difficult? Not easy? What is it, then?' So the man went to the daughter and asked her: 'Your father, your mother and

your brother all gave me different answers. Who is right?'

The daughter replied, 'If you make it difficult, it is difficult. If you make it easy, it is easy. But if you don't think, then the truth is just as it is. Where are "difficult" and "easy"? Only in the mind. Meditation is just as it is.'

Chapter 9

On Being Still

On the one hand, meditation is as simple as finding a quiet place to sit down, lowering or closing your eyes and watching your breath. It can be done in a cave as easily as on a park bench, in a church or a field, on a plane or a train. On the other hand, creating a peaceful environment is most conducive to developing a peaceful mind, especially in the early days, and finding the right kind of sitting posture is important as the body both responds to and affects the mind. So we have given special attention to these practicalities, knowing that it will be most beneficial for you when you are fully prepared to practise.

Timing Is Everything

We recommend that to start with you practise for at least fifteen minutes a day, and up to thirty if that feels comfortable. As you practise more you will start to know intuitively when you want to sit and for how long. It begins to speak to you and you find your own rhythm. Pay no attention if you hear other people extolling the virtues of their long sessions or special techniques. Just trust your own inner guidance.

Having said that, you may be doing less than you are capable of. Your session needs to be long enough to greet, meet and put down any distractions such as doubt, boredom, fantasy, impatience, anxiety and frustration. These are familiar problems that arise at some point in most sessions and it is easy to get swayed by any one of them to the point of stopping your meditation. If you have set yourself a time limit, such as thirty minutes, you will need to discipline yourself to stay there that long when distractions start to pull at you.

You may want to use an alarm clock, especially if you are on your own – but do choose one with a quiet ring so that it is not too startling. The advantages of doing so are, first, that you can really devote yourself to what you are doing instead of constantly checking the time, and, second, that it keeps you sitting there even if your mind is getting restless. Without a time limit it is easy to give up, whereas if you continue you will probably find the chattering becoming quieter and a deeper peace emerging. The clearest moments often come just before the end of a session. After a while you will not need an alarm – your body will become familiar with the timescale and you will simply know when the session is over.

Once this happens, you will find your meditation going deeper and becoming longer of its own accord. The average time that most people practice is thirty to forty minutes a day, sometimes twice a day. A few like to practise for up to an hour. More than that and your body will probably begin to feel quite tired, so it will need to stretch and move. During retreats or longer sessions of meditation, periods of sitting are interspersed with periods of walking meditation. This releases the tension in the body without distracting the mind.

As with relaxation, each person has their own preference about when to practise. Traditionally it is said that the hour before sunrise and the hour after sunset are the best. However, this does not always fit into our schedule! It is not advisable to meditate after eating a meal – too much energy is being used in digestion, which makes it more difficult to focus the mind. Besides, it is much harder to breathe freely when you have a full stomach! Find the time that works for you and stay with it. As discussed in Chapter 5, being disciplined about time makes it more likely that you will stick to a regular practice.

A Quiet Space

'*Finding a quiet space in a busy house is not easy. I have had to develop some ground rules, especially with my teenage son who will "forget" I am meditating, burst into the room, tut loudly and go out slamming the door. He then tells me afterwards that if I was meditating properly I wouldn't hear him!*'

Divya

Finding the right place to meditate is as important as finding the right time. If you create a special place to practise you will help your mind to understand that in this place, at this time, you go to the quiet space within. After a while the place itself takes on a familiar and supportive feeling: as soon as we sit down we feel ready to meditate, and there is a spaciousness that becomes associated with this one place. That is why churches, temples and other places of prayer or meditation have such a quiet and embracing feeling – the years of practice build up a respect and reverence for the divine that we can tangibly feel.

If you do not have a room that you can set aside for relaxation and meditation, see if you can find a corner in your bedroom or study which you can turn into a 'world within a world'. Create the right sitting place with your chair or cushions. Face a wall or a window with the curtains drawn rather than into the centre of the room, which can be too distracting. You may want to include a small table for flowers, a candle, precious objects or special books. Make this a place that respects and symbolises your inner world. It will soon become a powerful, self-renewing place of nourishment and harmony.

You can also meditate in any natural setting, such as by a river, in a meadow or wood or by the sea. You can meditate in busy places, but this may take a little more practice. It is certainly very grounding to focus on your breathing, perhaps counting your breaths, while travelling on a train or bus, but you might not want to close your eyes. If you are going to meditate outside, do be aware of potential unintended effects on other people. One man who just wanted to meditate on a mountain in North Wales found himself being unwillingly rescued by the Snowdonia Search and Rescue Team, who had been alerted by passing hikers of a strange man sitting on the hill. When the Rescue Team finally found him and told him they had come to rescue him, he replied that he was quite happy as he was, so the Rescue Team went back down the mountain and the man went back to his meditation!

Dressing for Comfort

You will find it easier to wear loose, comfortable clothing such as baggy cotton trousers – jeans or a tight skirt will make meditation much more difficult and will distract you. When we sit still for a period of time any little restriction soon grabs our attention. If you are wearing a belt or any other restrictive items, loosen or remove them before you start. Some people wear the same clothes each time they meditate, or perhaps have a shawl or blanket that they always use. Again, this is a way of building up associations that draw you into the meditative state. Do what feels right for you.

It is important to be warm enough. While we are meditating the whole body relaxes and slows down, so we can sometimes feel a bit chilly. A light blanket usually does the job, just keeping the draughts out. But make sure you are not too warm or you will soon be dropping off to sleep.

'I went to a Zen monastery in the north of England for a week of meditation practice. It was very cold and there was snow on the ground. The meditation hall was in a converted barn, and as the centre was relatively new there had not been time to do much building work. We sat in that hall with the wind whistling through the cracks in the barn walls, and snow sometimes got in too. It was freezing! I remember wearing gloves and a woollen hat. Yet as the week went on and our practice got deeper and quieter, I noticed the cold less. It wasn't that I was getting any physically warmer, but the more I went inward the less I noticed what was happening to my body. One day I came out of a long and deep meditation to find snow on me! I hadn't even noticed.'

Debbie

Posture Makes Perfect

Getting the right posture is, in many ways, the most important part of our preparation, for when we find the right posture the body moves into an inner stillness, whereas the wrong posture will cause continual distraction and physical discomfort. How we sit says a great deal about what is happening inside the mind – it is more than a posture, it is also an attitude. A slightly slumped back or rounded shoulders speak of lethargy, sleepiness, perhaps depression, sadness or grief; a rigid back denotes tension; crossed arms or ankles (when sitting in a chair) imply closedness or resistance. These are not qualities that we want to bring to our meditation. An upright back with a gently open chest implies personal dignity, wakefulness and presence; we are relaxed, yet also alert – perfect for meditation.

Try it for yourself. Experiment with different postures, and you will soon feel the difference in the effect on your mind. Even if your body is unable to sit straight, you can still maintain an alert and wakeful attitude. You are consciously coming to practise meditation and this is reflected in the subtle position of your body, whether sitting or even lying down. We honour our posture as the ground for our practice. 'The ideal state of tranquillity comes from experiencing body and mind being synchronised,' writes Chögyam Trungpa in *Shambhala*. 'If body and mind are unsynchronised, then your body will slump – and your mind will be elsewhere.... When mind and body are synchronised, then, because of your good posture, your breathing happens naturally; and because your breathing and your posture work together, your mind has a reference point to check back to.'

Sitting right

Meditation is best done in a seated position. If absolutely necessary it can be done lying down, but we associate lying with relaxing and sleeping, and meditation is neither of these. In the East, people traditionally squat, kneel or adopt a cross-legged posture, whereas in the West we have grown accustomed to sitting in armchairs and our legs do not get so easily into a crossed position. For those who are able, sitting on a cushion on the floor is the conventional posture. It is very grounded – there is a sense of being firmly rooted and in balance with the world. When the spine is in the right position it naturally supports itself with little effort, which minimises any stiffness; with a bent or unsupported back all our muscles have to work harder to keep it upright and they will soon be aching or hurting.

There are a number of variations of this posture that you can try: all that matters is which one works for you. There is no point in being in pain for fifteen minutes and at the same time trying to focus your attention on your practice – the pain will dominate. It is far more beneficial, especially in the early stages, to be comfortable so that you are free to focus inwards with less distraction. Even if you cannot yet get into a cross-legged position comfortably you can practise it, perhaps at times when you are not meditating. For instance, while you are watching TV or reading a book try sitting cross-legged for a while, easing and stretching your tight muscles. You can also do stretching and yoga exercises or t'ai chi. After a while it will become more natural and easier to hold for longer periods.

> 'When I first began meditation I would sit on the floor and my knees would be up by my ears. My legs were so stiff I thought I would never be able to get them down to the ground. It amazed me to see how, as I persevered, they slowly relaxed

and opened. Now I can sit cross-legged quite happily. We have become so stiff and unnatural in our movements that the body has forgotten its original aliveness.'

Eddie

It helps to experiment with the number of cushions you might need. To begin with you may want quite a pile to sit on before your knees are able to reach all the way down. The most important aspect of all the positions described below is that the buttocks should be higher than the knees as this enables the spine to relax in an upright position and the blood to flow more freely. If your knees are too high your back will curve and soon get very uncomfortable and tired, and your legs will get pins and needles; as a result you will feel distracted and lose your sense of alertness. Having a straight back also enables the breath to flow more easily, which helps your concentration.

As you go on you will probably find you need fewer cushions, until you just have one to lift the base of your spine into an upright, self-supporting position. Meditation pillows are available ready-made, or you can buy a piece of foam four to six inches thick, or you can make your own as described below. It is important that the cushion is fairly firm; if it is too soft it will not support your spine properly.

It also helps considerably to have a soft mat or folded blanket under your legs, creating a padding for your ankles and knees so that your joints do not get stressed. Instructions are given on pp. 137–8 for making a meditation pad from foam.

In the pictures you will see a variety of postures. Start with the ordinary cross-legged posture (fig. 1), then after a few weeks see if you can open your legs further and get your knees nearer the ground, as in the Burmese posture (fig. 2), in which one leg goes in front of the other. As you get to feel

fig. 1 Cross-legged posture   **fig. 2** Burmese posture

fig. 3 Half-lotus posture   **fig. 4** Japanese posture

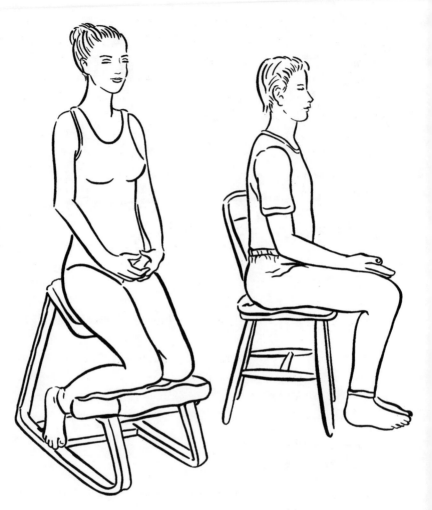

fig. 5 Kneeling chair   **fig. 6** Straight-backed chair

more comfortable with this posture you may want to try the half-lotus posture (fig. 3), in which one foot is lifted and rests on the calf of the other leg.

You may prefer to use a small wooden meditation stool which you can either buy or make yourself. It will help you sit in a kneeling position and takes all the pressure off your thighs. By being lifted a few inches off the ground, your back is well supported. This is known as the Japanese meditation position. Do ensure that you are kneeling on a folded blanket or mat of some sort, so as to take the weight off your shinbones and ankles. It helps to let your ankles hang over the back of the mat so that your feet are not being pushed backwards (fig. 4). An alternative to the meditation stool is the kneeling chair, readily available from many office and furniture stores (fig. 5).

If you are not comfortable sitting in the traditional cross-legged posture or kneeling, then a firm, straight-backed chair (see fig. 6) is fine. But it is just as important for your back to be upright, with your feet placed firmly on the floor, and your hands on your lap or thighs. No crossed legs or folded arms – your body needs to be at ease and relaxed. Note that when you are sitting in a chair it is much easier to nod off to sleep!

Try the different postures to see how you feel and how your meditation goes in each one. Only you can discover what is right for your body.

To make a meditation cushion
You will need:

- a length of tough cotton or canvas about eight feet long by seven inches wide
- two circles of the same cloth of ten-inch diameters
- lots of foam chips or kapok for stuffing

Pleat the long strip into one and a half inch pleats at two-inch intervals. Pin to the two circles, making sure there is a four-inch overlap at the ends. Sew and turn inside out. Stuff the cushion until it is the desired height for you to sit on comfortably.

To make a meditation pad
You will need:

- a piece of 24 × 36 inch foam one or two inches thick
- enough plain cotton material to cover it
- a zip, poppers or Velcro

Cover the foam with the material, attaching the zip, poppers or Velcro to one of the short sides so that you can remove the cover for washing.

To make a meditation stool
You will need:

- a plank of wood about ¾ inch thick, six inches wide and three feet long
- metal brackets, wooden pegs, screws or nails
- soft cloth or padding

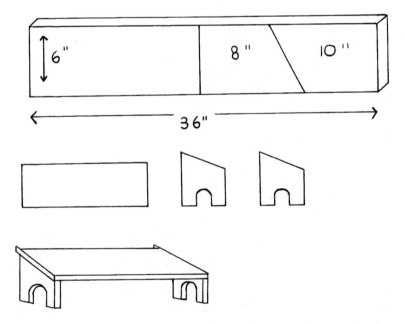

Saw the plank in two, then saw one of the pieces into two at an angle. Put the stool together with brackets, pegs, screws or nails so that the stool leans slightly forward. Finally, cover it with material, padding it first if you prefer.

Other body parts

Apart from your legs and spine, other body parts also affect your posture. As with the spine, the position of your hands can say a great deal about your inner feelings. Notice if you tend to clasp your hands together or scrunch them up, and then observe how it feels to open them into a more relaxed position. Or put them palms down and observe how it feels when you turn them palms up. Try letting your hands rest easily on your thighs, or bring them together in your lap, one on top of the other, with thumbs touching (fig. 7).

fig. 7 Hand position

It is important for your shoulders to be relaxed. Very often the weight of the arms can subtly pull down on the shoulder muscles, creating tiredness or tension. Slowly this will pull your back into a slumped position. This can easily be avoided either by using a cushion on your lap or by tying a scarf or sweater around your waist, on which to rest your hands. That way the arms are lifted slightly and the shoulders can naturally fall back, opening the chest and keeping the spine straight.

Your head should rest easily on your shoulders, tilting neither up nor down. Let it be completely natural, without any straining. Your eyes can be closed, or slightly open but looking downwards. Most people prefer to have their eyes closed because it is less distracting. But others go to sleep more easily in this position, so they like to keep their eyes half open. If you have your eyes open, lower your eyelids so that you can only see a few feet in front of you. Focus on one spot on the floor and let your eyes rest there. They will soon diffuse. Keep them in this resting, unseeing position so you do not get distracted by anything else around you.

Practice – Posture Perfect

When you first sit down, spend a few moments checking your posture and releasing any tension. Work upwards through your body.

- Are your legs comfortable and relaxed?
- Check the whole of your back. Move forwards and backwards a little to get a sense of balance and feel what a straight back is like. Bend forwards as far as you can, then gently come back up, head first, feeling your back straighten and lift as you do so.
- Release any tension in your shoulders. Let go of whatever burdens or responsibilities you are carrying. Make sure your shoulders are not being pulled down by your arms and hands – if necessary, lift your hands slightly by resting them on a cushion on your lap.
- Put your hands in your lap, one on top of the other, or rest them on your thighs.
- Your neck should be relaxed, with your head tilting neither up nor down but just resting comfortably.
- Take a deep breath and feel the poise, strength and dignity in your posture.

Aches and Pains

Whatever your position there are bound to be times when your body begins to ache – perhaps your back, your shoulders or your knees, or odd pains in different places. There is no point in being distracted by the pain while thinking you have to stay still no matter what. If you need to, just gently move a leg or release your shoulders to let go of any tension. You can do this while maintaining your focus. When the tension is gone or the blood has recirculated, simply move back into your original position. Sometimes the cushion or stool will cut off the circulation under your thighs; if so, you need to pad yourself with a blanket or extra cushion under your buttocks. Or it may occur where you have one ankle resting on the other; in this situation, simply open your legs a little further to release the pressure, or put a cushion under one knee. It is important to recognise where the body is being strained by being in the wrong position, which is demonstrated in pain that does not go away after the meditation but continues to ache. We are not trying to force the body into a new place but to let it open naturally into the position.

Pain can also be a way of being distracted from meditation, as if the body is purposely trying to draw us away from our concentration. When our focus is really clear we are not so easily affected by physical discomforts. Many a time people come out of a meditation session to find that their leg has gone to sleep without their noticing it.

'During a week of meditation, when we were sitting for long periods, my knees began to hurt very badly. By the third day I was rubbing in every form of heat-producing ointment and muscle relaxant I could find! By the fourth day I thought this is it: I shall either have to leave the programme or get through the pain. There is no other choice. We were not able to sit in *chairs, so I had to keep sitting on my cushion or leave. I decided to stay and to increase my concentration, to get as focused as I possibly could. As I did so I found my knees becoming less insistent. Somehow any pain that was there no longer penetrated my awareness. I had simply needed to relax more.'*

Debbie

Other aches and pains that occur may relate not to posture or physical problems but to issues arising in ourselves, indications that long-held psycho/emotional issues are being released as tensions in the body are relaxed. Areas like the chest or stomach that have been held tight against rejection or hurt, muscles tightened in defence or anger, knots of grief or remorse, or contractions of despair may all come to the surface, along with memories or associated feelings. This can be seen in a moment of intense pain that occurs while we are sitting but goes when we finish meditating.

Try not to contract against the pain. Breathe into it, softening any resistance. Take a few moments to enter into it, to let your non-judgemental mind simply be with the pain. Embrace it with compassion and softness. Feel the pain, relax into it. See if it has anything to tell you. See where it needs to go. You may find layer after layer being released. Let it go. Do not judge yourself, just honour whatever arises.

Monkey Mind

'When I was meditating I soon realised I was just sitting and thinking. And my back ached, or I felt as if ants were crawling all over me. My body really complained, my knees ached, I got pins and needles, and I wanted to eat something!'

Margaret

While you are meditating you are bound to experience distractions. This is normal. Your thoughts will distract you, your body with its aches and pains will distract you, as will a dog barking, the sound of traffic or a neighbour shouting. Your mind is like a monkey leaping from branch to branch, tree to tree, forever grasping and playing. But as you persevere your mind will slowly get used to the stillness and begin to settle.

The biggest mistake is to think that meditation is immediately going to create this wonderfully peaceful state. However, we cannot catch the wind any more than we can force the mind to be still. Distraction is so normal that it is not to be concerned about. Do not get impatient with yourself or believe that this proves you cannot meditate. In the early stages it is rare to get more than a few moments of clear concentration, and even after many years you can still find your mind going off in all directions. It is quite common for the mind to lose focus hundreds of times in a single session.

Any resistance, such as feelings of guilt, inadequacy or hopelessness, will only make matters worse. When you stop resisting, the thoughts will stop distracting. Each time you become aware of distraction, just let go of the thoughts and come back to the practice. One way to deal with thoughts is to see them as birds in the sky and just let them fly away. A student of ours told us she had given each type of thought a different-coloured bird – fear was yellow, anger was red, envy was green, and so on. In this way she could label the thought as a colour and was less distracted by it. Or you can just label them 'thinking', repeating the word gently until the thought subsides and you can come back to your practice.

All sorts of things will arise and pass away as long as you do not hold on to them. Remember, the content of the thoughts is not important, do not take them too seriously or identify with them as making you either a terrible, evil person or a wonderful, generous person. Just see it all as a monkey trying to get your attention. Come back to your practice, to the focus of your meditation, and use that as an anchor between your thoughts.

Two aspects of the monkey mind that are most difficult to deal with are judgement and criticism. We judge ourselves, our practice, our progress or lack of it, other people's posture or lack of mindfulness; we criticise ourselves, the teacher, the technique, the cushion – the list is endless! It is easy to slip into judgement and criticism, especially if you are trying really hard and do not feel you are getting anywhere. But the more you judge, the sooner you will stop practising altogether.

A number of teachers have a simple method of dealing with this problem, and that is to count each time you catch yourself being judgemental or critical: 'Judgement number one ... judgement number two ...' and so on. Not only will it make you laugh at your own mind – especially when you get into the hundreds – but it will also make you very aware of your mental patterns. Soon you won't need much help in being generous and compassionate to both yourself and others.

It is the identification with the thought that gives it energy. Immediately you identify with the thought you have lost the ability just to see or witness. Instead of saying, 'I am uncomfortable' or 'I am hungry/bored/irritated', try transforming it to just seeing that there is a lack of comfort or observing that there is hunger, boredom, irrtation. This creates a space between you and the thought. Or you can try saying, 'Let it go' or 'Let go, let God.' Even stronger is to repeat to yourself, 'Put it down.' As a last resort, try repeating the Pali word *Atammayata* over and over until the thought has gone. In plain English it means, 'I ain't going to mess with you no more!'

If strong or deeply held feelings arise, or ones that do deserve attention, acknowledge this. Then take that thought or feeling and metaphorically put it outside yourself, perhaps six inches away from you or beyond the edge of your mat. Visualise yourself doing this. At the same time as acknowledging the issue, confirm that you will come back to deal with it after the meditation session is over. Putting it outside your space in this way acknowledges its importance but means that you do not have to go into it now. Very often, when you do come to deal with it, the feeling has either diminished or begun to resolve itself.

Remember, this is a practice, and you are not expected to get it right every time! Great patience is needed for anything new, especially where your own mind is concerned. Be gentle on yourself, be kind to yourself; your meditation is not your enemy but is there to serve you, to befriend you. The more you can focus on the breathing and simply being in the present moment, the more your concentration will grow and the monkey will tire. Try watching the breath so closely that you watch the beginning, middle and end of the breath. You see the difference between the inhalation and the exhalation. You become the breath. Then see if you can find where your thoughts have gone.

Zzzzzzzzzz

It is quite common to find yourself getting sleepy during meditation, especially if you are doing it in the evening after a day at work. Try changing the time you practise – do it every morning for a week and see what difference this makes. Ensure your posture is right and especially that you have a straight back, as a rounded back will add to your drowsiness. Change your posture by moving your legs, and take a few deep breaths; or keep your eyes open throughout. Or alternate walking meditation and sitting meditation every fifteen minutes. All of this will help you become more alert.

At other times sleepiness will overcome us if issues are arising that we are reluctant to deal with – sleeping can be an unconscious way of avoiding ourselves. Look beneath the sleepiness and ask yourself if there are other issues in need of attention – fear, sadness, depression. The effort required to stay concentrated and alert has to come from you. Try saying to yourself, 'Just this breath', and staying with each breath only as long as that one breath – and then the next breath – and then the next one, moving awareness closer and closer to this present moment.

Practice – Breathing In, Breathing Out

Find a comfortable place to sit with your back straight and your chest open and relaxed. Spend a few moments feeling gratitude for your body, your seat and the world around you. Sitting quietly, with your eyes closed, take a deep breath and let it out through your mouth.

Now bring your awareness to your breath – to the flow of your breath as it enters and leaves your body. Let your attention naturally focus on the nose, the chest or the belly, depending on where you most easily observe your breath. Just watch the flow of the breath, noting the texture, temperature and feel of each breath and the rise and fall of your body.

Now begin to repeat silently, 'Breathing in I relax my body, breathing out I relax my mind.' Repeat these words with every in and out breath for as long as you want. After a while you can simply repeat, 'Breathing in, breathing out' with each in and out breath. If thoughts or distractions pull your attention away just see them as birds in the sky and let them fly away, always coming back to your breath.

Take note of how the breath comes in and then leaves again. Through the breath we are connected to all beings. When you are ready to finish, take a deep breath and let it out slowly through your mouth. Take a moment to honour your inter-connectedness and dedicate the practice to the benefit of all beings. Then gently open your eyes.

Chapter 10

Many Paths
Up the Mountain

This chapter includes seven main forms of meditation with detailed descriptions for practice. You may wish to record these practices on to a tape to play back to yourself, or have a friend read them. Alternatively, meditation tapes are available from the address on p.174.

We all differ in our needs and capabilities, so it is important that you try these practices to find the one which is most suitable for you. We recommend you to start with the Breath Awareness Meditation and/or the Witness Meditation. These are really the most fundamental of all meditations, used throughout many religious and spiritual traditions because they develop concentration, objectivity and stillness, allowing a natural awareness and insight to arise. However, not everyone is suited to these two practices, so if you do not feel at ease we recommend you either use a mantra or sound, as in the Mantra Meditation, or use your sight as in the Candle Gazing Meditation. These latter two practices use the senses to draw the attention inwards.

Mantra Meditation is particularly good if you are in a state of agitation or your thoughts are running wild. It is like a broom sweeping the mind clean!

The Metta and Forgiveness Meditations work specifically with our feelings and with developing more altruistic qualities. Start with the Metta Meditation before coming to the Forgiveness Meditation; in that way you will establish a foundation of compassion and loving kindness in which to embrace forgiveness. Metta is particularly helpful for opening the heart, awakening a love for ourselves and releasing any resistance towards others.

Use the Walking Meditation at any time, anywhere. It is a wonderful practice that can be adapted to suit your needs – fast or slow, inside or out.

Remember, before you begin a practice session, to spend time relaxing so that you feel physically supple and at ease. You might do the Instant ICR described on p.78, some yoga or stretching and deep breathing, or a body scan as described on p.18.

Beginning and Ending

It is important to be conscious of the beginning and ending of meditation, to create a moment of awareness. You may want to recite a short prayer or blessing, or a few words that bring you into the moment, such as 'My body is relaxed and easy, my mind is quiet and peaceful, my heart is open and loving.' Or you can enter into a place of gratitude and thankfulness by saying: 'I feel gratitude for the cushion [stool/chair] I am sitting on and for the ground beneath me that support me in my practice; for the room around me that protects me and holds me safe. I feel gratitude for my body that enables me to sit in stillness; and for the breath that gives me life.'

As you finish your practice, before you get up, spend a few moments in awareness of what has happened, creating any form of closing that feels appropriate for you. For instance, you can offer your practice to the benefit of all beings by saying: 'I offer the merits of this practice that all beings may be free from suffering.' In this way you are honouring that whatever you do affects both yourself and others due to your inter-connected relationship with all beings. Or you may prefer to say something like, 'May all beings reside in calmness of mind and openness of heart', or 'May all beings live in peace/harmony/joy'.

Breathing Meditation

Watching the breath – simply watching it enter and leave the body – is one of the oldest and most trusted forms of meditation practice. The rhythm of the breath is the flow of all life: it is constant and steady and has a naturally inward action. By focusing on it we internalise our attention and deepen our awareness.

When you come to practise, you need to first relax and quieten your body so that your breath flows smoothly. Then you need to make friends with the breath, to feel an easefulness in breathing. As the action of breathing is done automatically it can, to begin with, feel very strange and unnatural to be focusing on it: you may find yourself trying to control the process, breathing more quickly or more slowly. So you have to learn how to just watch, to bring awareness to your natural rhythm, to witness the depth and length of each breath.

Find the place where you are most in touch with the breath. This may be at the tip of the nose, where the breath enters; it may be in the centre of the chest – the heartspace;

or it may be lower down in the abdomen, an inch or so beneath the navel. You are looking for the place where you best focus attention on the flow of the breath. Then stay with that place for the duration of the meditation. And from that place just watch the rise and fall, the in and out, of each breath. Follow the breath so you are aware of every movement and change.

As each breath is new, fresh and different, so it keeps you present. The rhythm may change, and the length or depth of each breath may change throughout the practice – that is normal. The object of breath awareness meditation is simply to be aware, to observe, to watch the breath as it is without trying to interfere or change it. The breath then becomes an anchor that holds you focused. It is always there to return to in between thoughts or distractions. In this way it becomes your greatest friend.

As we practise we soon find that we are flowing with the breath, merging with it, dissolving into the rhythm and flow. The breath internalises our attention, brings our awareness into ourselves and then embodies that awareness as we focus deeper into the breathing itself, until it is as if we are no longer observing the breath but our being breathed. The in and out rhythm of the breath is the rhythm of all life, the rhythm of the rising and passing of all phenomena.

> '*An experience which was deeply moving was when I had been watching my breathing for perhaps ten or fifteen minutes and I suddenly became aware that I didn't know if I was breathing in or out. It was as though I was just a part of the breath, or that the breath was being breathed through me.*'
>
> Barbara

There are many different forms of breath meditation. The best way to start is just to become aware of the breath by bringing your attention to where we most connect with it. At that place, rest your mind and simply watch the movement of the breath and the body as the breath enters and leaves. Then you can count the breaths, as described in detail in the longer practice below. Alternatively, as you focus on the breath coming in and going out you can silently repeat. 'Breathing in ... breathing out', with each breath, as in the practice on p.147.

If your mind seems particularly distracted and you need extra focusing, combine counting each breath with the 'Breathing in, breathing out' words. Do this by silently repeating 'Breathing in ... one ... breathing out. Breathing in ... two ... breathing out', and so on up to ten, then start at one again. Just learning to hold the concentration through ten numbers is a feat in itself! If your mind is at ease, you can simply use the words 'In ... out' with each breath, or just watch the flow of the breath without any words. The words are there to help you hold your attention steady, like an anchor. If you do not need them, just sit watching the breath.

Another form of breathing meditation is known as *Anapanasati*. There are quite a few stages to this practice, but it starts by becoming aware of the breath as it enters the nostrils. After a few minutes you move the focus of attention down to your navel and watch the breath from there for a few minutes. Then you bring these two places together by paying attention to the flow of the breath between the tip of your nose and your navel. Silently repeat, 'Nose tip to navel ... navel to nose tip' while following the flow of each in and out breath. This keeps the mind focused on the movement of the breath, while internalising the attention deeper into the body. In that way we develop a greater awareness and stability.

Remember, there are bound to be distractions! Know that this will happen so you do not feel like a failure. Simply label the thoughts as thoughts, the distractions as distractions and come back to the breath.

Practice – Breath Awareness Meditation

Start by finding a comfortable seated position with your hands resting in your lap or on your thighs and your eyes closed or lowered. Take a deep breath and feel at ease in your posture. Spend a few moments developing an appreciation and gratitude for your seat, for the ground beneath you, for the building around you, for your body, and for the breath as it enters and leaves.

With this practice your breath is completely natural – not forced, hurried, slow or heavy. Attention is focused on the flow of the breath, watching it come into the body and leave again. Find the place in your body that feels most natural to your attention – either the belly area approximately two inches below the navel, or the area of the heartspace in the centre of your chest, or the tip of the nose.

Now start counting your breaths. Do this by silently counting at the end of each out breath. Breathe in, breathe out and count one. Breathe in, breathe out and count two. Breathe in, breathe out and count three. Continue in this way until you reach ten and then start at one again, counting one number at the end of each out breath.

If you lose the counting, or find yourself counting beyond ten just bring your attention back and start at one again. Use the counting as an anchor to keep your mind focused on the breath. Stay in the present by breathing just one breath fully. Then breathing another. Then another.

The mind is easily distracted, wanting to go in different directions. Notice any thoughts, label them 'thinking' and let them go. See them as birds in the sky that fly away. Keep coming back to the counting. As you continue the counting, your mind will become quieter and your sense of the world around you will withdraw into the silence of your own being.

After about ten minutes, change to counting silently at the beginning of each in breath. Count one, breathe in, breathe out. Count two, breathe in, breathe out. Count three, breathe in, breathe out. Continue up to ten and then start back at one. This shifts the focus of your concentration from awareness of the breath *after* you have breathed to becoming aware of the breath *before* it enters the body.

You are now having to concentrate more deeply. No matter what distractions may be going on, keep your mind focused and at one with the rhythm of the breath, which is the universal rhythm of the tides, the winds, the seasons. The breath is a part of this rhythm and is your connection to all life.

After about ten minutes stop the counting and simply watch the in and out flow of the breath. As you do this, your individual self begins to dissolve into the breath, as if you are being breathed. The breath gives us life but it is not ours to own, only to share.

After a further ten minutes, or longer if you want, gently come back into yourself, becoming aware of the seat beneath you, the room you are in and the world outside your room. You may like to dedicate the benefits of this practice to all beings or simply feel thanks.

Witness Meditation

The witness state is one in which we observe or witness ourselves without getting personally involved in anything that is going on. This form of meditation is deceptively simple. On the one hand all we are doing is witnessing ourselves – whether it is our breath, thoughts, feelings or body – and just being with whatever arises. On the other hand, as soon as we pay attention to ourselves in this way we tend to be drawn into the dramas, scenarios, aches and pains that are constantly there, enticing us away from such objectivity and into subjectivity.

So the witness practice is very revealing. It is like a mirror, showing us how discursive our minds are. It is also a very grounding and centring practice as we are developing awareness of our whole being just as it is – this means we are being fully present. In this practice we just sit, with no direct object of our concentration other than ourselves. We sit with ourselves and allow whatever arises to arise. Without clinging to it or developing it further, we just watch and pay attention. Our thoughts come and go, we see them just passing through without developing them into further thoughts. Our feelings arise and we observe without attachment. We are simply being with ourselves. By doing this we gain the insight that who we are is not just the impermanent, fleeting experiences, but something more.

Practice – Witness Meditation

Start by getting into a comfortable seated position with your hands in your lap or on your thighs and your eyes closed or lowered. Take a deep breath and feel at ease in your posture. Spend a few moments developing appreciation and gratitude for your environment and for your breath.

Bring your awareness to your body. Witness your body sitting for meditation. Let your mind move through your body, slowly registering each part, starting at the toes. Witness how your toes feel, and the rest of your feet ... witness your legs ... knees and thighs. Simply being aware, observing them as they are. Bring that awareness up your body ... the buttocks ... lower back ... middle back and upper back. Witness the whole of your back and how it feels. Then observe your pelvis and belly ... your abdomen and chest. Take a deep breath and watch how your body moves with the breath. Then observe your fingers and hands ... arms ... elbows and shoulders. Experience whatever they feel like. Observe your neck ... jaw ... mouth ... nose ... eyes ... ears ... forehead ... and the rest of your head. Simply witness yourself as you are.

Now become aware of the natural flow of the in and out breath ... witness the flow of the ordinary breath. Observe the breath in all its detail. Watch where it comes into your body and how that feels. Watch the movement of the body and where the breath goes. Watch how the body feels as the breath fills it and then leaves. Watch the moments between the breaths and stay with this for a few minutes.

Now become aware of your thoughts and witness them ... just let them spontaneously arise, whatever they are. Whether they are good or bad does not matter, just be a witness and observe your thoughts. Do not get involved, but maintain the observation ... see how your thoughts arise like a picture on a screen. Watch your feelings arise. Notice if they have an effect on your body. Notice if one thought or feeling leads to another. Be a witness to yourself.

Now externalise your awareness. Become like radar

and send your awareness outside of you into the room you are in ... then out into the street ... further and further ... become aware of all the sounds but do not identify with any one particular sound ... just witness the sounds of life ... stay with this for a few minutes. Become as acutely aware as you can, observing whatever you hear without judgement.

Now bring your awareness in and once again become the witness of your thoughts ... let them spontaneously arise ... whatever the quality of your thinking is not important ... do not get involved ... just be the witness ... the more you are able to maintain the witness and stay detached the more you will see these thoughts just as thoughts.

Now become aware of the breath in your nostrils ... feel as if you are in the nostrils ... watching the breath from the tip of the nose to the space between your eyebrows like a triangle with no base ... breathing in and out ... getting closer and closer to the breath ... if the mind drifts bring it back to the breath.

Now become aware of the eyebrow centre ... and observe a tiny dot of light ... the size of a pinpoint ... keep the gaze steady and one-pointed ... as you witness the pinpoint of light watch it open ... feel the peace and joy of your own true self ... let the whole of your being be filled with light. Stay with this for a few minutes.

Take a few moments to become aware of your breathing, your body and the room around you. Take a deep breath. You may like to dedicate the benefits of this practice to all beings or simply feel thanks.

Mantra Meditation

Mantra means a sacred word and is composed of two elements, repetition and freedom, implying that through repetition we find our freedom. Mantra meditation consists of repeating a sound or series of sounds over and again. This is also known as *Japa*. You can do this silently, intoning the sound in your mind, or you can repeat it out loud when you are alone – this is good if your mind is particularly active. The purpose is to become so absorbed in the sound that the mind becomes completely quiet. It has a powerful and purifying effect and can result in very deep absorption. Mantra meditation uses the language that the mind is familiar with – words or sounds – so that the mind does not rebel, while using them in such a repetitive way that the mind has nothing to cling to.

Most mantras are in the ancient Indian language of Sanskrit, as these sounds were first recognised as having deeply calming and beneficial effects. They were realised by the yogis while absorbed in deep meditation. The sound is aimed at awakening the divine potential that lies dormant in us all, and the meaning of the words is secondary to the effect. Any name of God or a word that helps you can be used. The most universal one-word mantra is 'Om', meaning God or the sound of the universe. It is pronounced with a long 'o' and a hummed 'm', stretched out so that the sound goes from the back of your throat to the front of your mouth. Other well-known mantras are 'Hari Om', 'So Hum', 'Om Ah' and 'Om Shanti', and ones that are not in Sanskrit such as Shalom, Allah, Hallelujah or Mother Mary. Amongst longer mantras is the Buddhist one *Om Mani Padme Hum*, which means Jewel in the Heart of the Lotus, indicating the potential that we all have for enlightenment – the sleeping Buddha or jewel within each one of us. And there is the well-loved Hindu mantra *Om Namah Shivaya*, meaning Homage to Shiva, the destroyer of ignorant or unenlightened energy. In Hinduism, Shiva is another name for God. Using mantra as meditation is also a form of *Bhakti*, or devotion. It is a practice of the heart that opens us to receiving the divine into our lives.

Practice – Mantra Meditation

Start the meditation by sitting in a normal meditation posture, relaxing your body and letting your breath settle. Then focus on the sound and begin either to repeat it silently or to intone it out loud. Stay with one mantra for the length of the practice. When using a single or two-word mantra, you can repeat it rhythmically with the in and out breath. Like the breath, the mantra acts as an anchor to hold the mind, to bring it to one point. It is a wonderful way of freeing the mind from confusion and doubt, and also of opening your heart. All you do is keep repeating that sound over and over, and watch what happens. Watch yourself becoming more and more deeply absorbed.

In order to increase concentration you can use a *mala* or string of either 27 or 108 beads (108 refers to the 108 Hindu names of God). Hold the mala in your right hand and rest the beads on your middle finger. Use your thumb to move one bead at a time towards you with each recitation of the mantra, as in the illustration opposite.

Prayer

Prayer is another form of devotional meditation, in which we focus on drawing ever closer to the divine through our

fig. 8 Using a mala

supplication. Prayer brings us to a place of deep humility and surrender, a letting go of the ego. Through prayer we experience the bliss of union with all creation, while the heart fills with God's love. As you sit quietly, allow prayer to arise spontaneously and freely, a natural response of the open heart. Or repeat the prayer below, written by Rev. Miranda Holden.

Finding Strength
May I find the strength within me to break free of all limitations
May I find the heart within me to be truly honest
May I find the courage within me to step into the light

May I find the nobility within me to treat myself and all others with compassion
May I find the wisdom within me to be still and listen
May I find the love within me to forgive myself and others
May I find the peace within me to give up my judgements
May I find the joy within me to celebrate all that is true, and surrender to the Divine all that is not.

Candle Gazing Meditation

Known as *Tratak* in yoga practices, this meditation uses focusing on a candle flame to bring the mind into concentrated one-pointedness. In place of a candle you could use an object such as a flower, a sacred image or icon, or a picture such as a mandala or simple geometric pattern.

Practice – Candle Gazing Meditation

Sit opposite a lighted candle, which should be two to three feet in front of you and the flame at eye level when your eyes are slightly lowered. It is best if there are no draughts to disturb the flame. Sitting quietly and focusing on the rhythm of your breath, gently gaze at the candle flame, if possible without blinking. After a few minutes, close your eyes and focus on re-creating the image of the flame in the area that is known as your third eye or wisdom centre – the space behind the centre of your eyebrows. After a few minutes repeat this procedure: watching, then re-creating the image inside. Continue for as long as it feels comfortable. As your concentration deepens, so the internal candle flame will burn more brightly. Your mind will become concentrated and increasingly one-pointed.

Metta Meditation

Heart-centred meditations are less concerned with developing one-pointed concentration than with developing qualities such as loving kindness, forgiveness or compassion. When we bring our attention wholeheartedly to contemplating loving kindness, for example, we begin to go beyond our mental preconceptions and even beyond loving thoughts into the actual experience of the feeling. We become loving, it is no longer separate to us. As love opens the heart so forgiveness naturally enters, as do compassion and the wish for all beings to be free from suffering.

The practice of Metta or loving kindness has been taught since the days of the Buddha as the most important way to open the heart to the power of love. It begins by bringing the focus of our attention to the area of the heart, as this is where we can most deeply connect with the actual feeling or experience of loving kindness as opposed to just the concept. For loving kindness is not rational or logical, it arises from within the depth of our being as we heal and release that which is holding us back from loving more fully. We soften resistance with the in and out breath, breathing out any tension, breathing in easefulness.

In this meditation you discover that to develop unconditional love you have to start by loving yourself, just as you are. This is not always easy, but it is essential. It is not something that will happen all at once, but we can start by acknowledging and accepting just one piece at a time, bringing warmth and tenderness to ourselves. We need to look at what is stopping us from loving ourselves and be at peace with what we find. In this first stage of the practice feelings often arise that we do not deserve happiness, do not deserve to be well. It is important to accept this negating aspect of ourselves that focuses on what we have done wrong or denies our true beauty, but also to pay it no great attention, always coming back to the practice.

Then we begin to include others in our practice, starting with our family and loved ones, followed by our dearest friends, bringing each one into our heart and embracing them with our loving kindness. Slowly the feeling grows inside, the heart feels as if it is opening and expanding. From there we go on to include people with whom we are in conflict, with whom there are difficulties or a breakdown in communication. This can be very hard, but the love we have already begun to feel will help us open to embracing such people into our heart. Here we begin to recognise that there is truly no difference between us – we each share the same breath and walk the same earth. The development of true equanimity enables us to see all beings as equal, ourselves included. The practice ends with expanding our loving kind-ness outwards towards all beings, in all directions, whoever they may be, wherever they may be. This takes us beyond the personal expressions of love into a universal experience of loving; a loving that does not need a specific object but loves simply because that is its nature.

Practice – Metta Meditation

The aim of this meditation is to develop a deeper experience of unconditional love and kindness. Start by finding a comfortable sitting position and close or lower your eyes. Spend a few moments developing appreciation and gratitude for yourself and your environment.

Bring the focus of your attention to the area of your heart and breathe into the heartspace in the centre of your chest. Focus on your breathing for a few minutes, gently watching the in and out flow of the breath and becoming one with this flow. Then visualise in your heart an image of yourself as you are, or repeat your name, or simply feel your presence there. Hold yourself in your heart as a mother would hold a child – gently and tenderly. Then silently repeat to yourself, 'May I be well, may I be happy, may I be filled with loving kindness.' Keep repeating these words in your heart.

As you do this, acknowledge any opposing thoughts that might arise – reasons why you should not be happy, or not be well, feelings of guilt or shame, of not being worthy of such love, or your inability to receive. Acknowledge these and then let them go. Continue repeating, 'May I be well, may I be happy, may I be filled with loving kindness.'

Breathe in love and kindness on your in breath, let go of any tension on your out breath. Embrace yourself, wish yourself wellness, happiness and peace. Accept yourself completely as you are, love yourself completely as you are. Deepen your appreciation and love for yourself. Breathe into your heart, opening more with each breath. Stay with this for a few minutes.

Now begin to expand your love further by bringing into your heart those relatives or friends whom you love. One by one bring them into your heart, visualising each one or repeating their name. Let them know how you feel, share your love with these precious beings. Silently repeat, 'May you be well, may you be happy, may you be filled with loving kindness.'

Breathing into your heart, wish them happiness, open yourself to loving kindness and forgiveness, letting go of any differences and embracing your connectedness. See how each of you is connected to each other, reflecting the beauty that each has to offer. Release the hold on any difficulties there may have been between you, any differences of opinion, anything that needs to be forgiven. Open your heart so you can embrace each one. 'I love you and I forgive you. I love you and I forgive you.' Stay with this for a few minutes.

Now feel your heart reaching out with love and acceptance towards someone with whom you are experiencing conflict. This may be a relative, friend or colleague – anyone with whom all is not right. Bring this person into your heart and begin to expand your loving kindness and compassion even to them. Let your acceptance, love and forgiveness flow towards this person. Silently repeat, 'May you be well, may you be happy, may you be filled with loving kindness.'

Breathe out any tension, and let the love in your heart reach out to this person. Remember that pain and hurt and anger are the result of forgetting our essential inter-connectedness – we pull back and close our hearts to each other. Open your heart now, reaching deeper to find forgiveness for this person and for yourself. Release the differences between you and rejoice in the connectedness. 'May you be well, may you be happy, may you be filled with loving kindness.' Stay with this for a few minutes.

Now begin to expand your loving kindness even further, outwards to all other beings. Slowly your love radiates outwards, like the ripples on a pond, reaching out towards all beings in all directions, realising that there is no difference between yourself and others. Your heart opens to all beings everywhere, whoever they may be. 'May all beings be well, may all beings be happy, may all beings be filled with loving kindness.'

Seek out any prejudice you may hold, any resistance towards others. Breathe into that resistance and let it go. Let your love reach into the prisons as much as the holy places. Every being on this planet is worthy of your love, whoever they may be. Bring light to those in darkness, love to those in need. Feel your love for all beings, unconditionally. Feel your connectedness with all beings, for ultimately we are all one. 'May all beings be at peace and may I be at peace with all beings.'

Now bring your awareness back to yourself in your heart. Feel love radiating throughout your whole being. Dissolve into this love. Know that as much love as you give to others, so even more will fill your being. Just as the flame of a candle can light a thousand other flames without losing its own flame, so your love can reach out to all beings and you will always be in a state of love. Breathing into your heart, this love knows no barriers, no limitations; it goes beyond all conditions. This is what you were born to know.

As you gently come out of this meditation, feel that love filling you with joy and bringing a smile to your face. This is true happiness, unconditional and free. May all beings live in peace and joy.

Forgiveness Meditation

Another, equallly important, heart-centred meditation is the development of forgiveness. This can be difficult to prac-tise, but very powerful. The meditation starts with forgiving ourselves first, then moves to forgiving someone who has hurt us, then to asking for forgiveness from someone we have hurt.

Forgiveness is a true opening of the heart, a surrendering of our hurt pride and wounded feelings. The beauty of forgiveness is the freedom it releases – the freedom to love, to give, to care. No longer are we locked into fear or anger. However, we do advise you to be clear about your feelings before beginning a forgiveness meditation practice. It may be necessary to really acknowledge how you feel and to know you are ready to let go, or else the practice may become a way of repressing your feelings rather than healing them. Remember, we do not have to forgive the act but we can forgive the person.

This practice teaches us that forgiveness is a gift to ourselves more than to anyone else, for it is in our own hearts that the release takes place. The other person may not know, he or she may not even be alive, yet we can let go of the hold they have over us, let go of the need for revenge, the feelings of guilt or shame. Doing so brings us powerfully into the present as it releases the past.

Practice – Forgiveness Meditation

Start by finding a comfortable sitting position and close or lower your eyes. Spend a few moments developing appreciation and gratitude.

Then bring your awareness to the breath as it enters and leaves your body, focusing on the area of your heart. With each out breath feel any tension or stress leaving; with each in breath feel quietness and openness growing and expanding in you. Relax and soften your heart.

Then bring an image or thought of yourself into that area. Visualise and hold yourself there, with gentleness. As you do so, become aware of forgiveness and begin to open to forgiving yourself. Silently and slowly repeat the words, 'I forgive myself. I forgive myself. For any harm I have done, for any pain I have caused, whether through my words or my actions, I forgive myself.'

Keep repeating these words. As you do so, all sorts of resistance may arise, all the reasons why you should not be forgiven; or all the things you have done that are unworthy, and all the shameful or guilty feelings associated with these things. Breathe into these memories and resistances, acknowledge them and let them go. Whatever arises is fine, but do not get involved. It is important to continue repeating the words and generating forgiveness. Release any resistances with your out breath. Come back to forgiveness with your in breath.

Let the forgiveness fill your entire being. Hold your-self in your heart as a mother would hold her child, tenderly, gently, with complete acceptance. Feel the forgiveness wash through your whole being. Keep repeating, 'I forgive myself.' Stay with this for a few minutes.

Now bring into your heart someone who needs to be forgiven by you, someone you would like to forgive. Hold this person in your heart. Feel their presence. Breathe into any feelings that arise; breathe out any anger, pain or fear and breathe in forgiveness. Soften your belly, let go of resistance.

Silently say to this person, 'I forgive you. I forgive you. For the harm you have inflicted and the pain you have caused, through your words and your actions, I forgive you.'

At first it may be difficult to forgive, but every step is a step towards healing. Take your time, keep repeating the words, keep breathing into your heart.

Recognise what is holding you back and let it go on each out breath ... breathe out all the reasons they should not be forgiven, all the times they have hurt you, and breathe in forgiveness. As you forgive, the boundaries between you begin to dissolve. Hold this person in your heart, feel your forgiveness embracing them, loving them. Silently repeat, 'I forgive you.' Stay with this for a few minutes.

Now bring into your heart someone from whom you wish to ask for forgiveness, someone you may have wronged or who has been hurt by you and has therefore closed their heart to you. Bring this person into your heart and hold them there with love and forgiveness. Silently repeat the words, 'I ask for your forgiveness. I ask for your forgiveness. If I have hurt you or caused you pain, through my words or my actions, please forgive me.'

Breathe into any resistance you may feel, breathe into the resentment, the hurt, the pain. Accept your own vulnerability and mistakes. Breathe out resistance and breathe in forgiveness. Keep repeating the words. As the forgiveness grows, let it pour through you. Feel your heart opening to forgiveness. Know that you are forgiven, that forgiveness is being given to you. Allow yourself to be forgiven. Repeat, 'I am forgiven.' Stay with this for a few minutes.

Now come back to yourself in your heart. Feel the joy of forgiveness in every part of your being. You are forgiven. You have forgiven. You have been forgiven. Let the release and the gratitude pour through you. Let the love that is within you radiate throughout your entire being. Rejoice in the forgiveness!

May all beings live in love. Take a deep breath of gratitude before closing your meditation.

Walking Meditation

'Walking meditation brings me into the present moment. As I walk I am not subject to whatever arises in my mind – thoughts or distractions dissolve into each step, each movement. I feel a connectedness to the ground and through that to all that exists. I feel supported by the ground beneath me. There is no path to follow, I am walking just to walk, with myself yet also with all things.'

Eddie

Like breathing, walking is something we do every day without any thought: we just walk and do our thinking or shopping or talking at the same time. Walking meditation is different. We are purposely not trying to get anywhere, and we are only doing one thing at a time, with full awareness. It is a way of moving and expanding awareness without losing our concentration. It creates a bridge between our sitting practice and our everyday life.

In walking meditation we are aware of each movement. It is the ideal balance to sitting meditation – in most traditions each period of sitting meditation, perhaps thirty minutes, is followed by a period of fifteen to thirty minutes of walking meditation, giving the body time to stretch and ease any sleepiness and the mind the opportunity to bring its focus from stillness to a moving object. This requires a different kind of concentration, one that can balance awareness of the external world with the rhythm of the breath and the movement. Walking meditation can be done inside or outside, in bare feet or in shoes. It can be done as one continual walk; or else locate two points about thirty paces apart (such as two trees) and walk to and fro between them. It can be done slowly or quickly, depending on your body's needs. The idea is to maintain awareness of the breath while also bringing awareness to the movement of the body, being fully present with the movement, with each single step.

> 'Breathing and walking. Breathing and walking. Watching the flow of the in and out breath, I walk, lifting, moving, placing. From one coconut tree to the next, then back again, the ground between is soft. Eyes downcast, I place my bare foot carefully, mindful of the black ants, spiders and beetles, not wishing to cause harm. Around me I am vaguely aware of others doing the same, breathing and walking, each in their own spaciousness.'
>
> Debbie

Walking meditation can also be done going down the street, along a beach, in the supermarket – wherever your feet take you. When done outside of formal practice it is mindful walking – awareness of the world and the movement of your body together. This mindfulness brings great presence to all our movements, not just walking. It maintains awareness of the inter-connectedness between the body, the earth and the environment. It is especially valuable if you are rushing or getting impatient!

Practice – Walking Meditation

Start by standing straight. Bring your left hand to your abdomen in a softly closed position, then cover it with your right hand. Keep this position, so that your arms are relaxed and not pulling on your shoulders. Your head should be steady, with your eyes open but looking at the ground only three to five feet in front of you. You need to see where you are going and to be aware of your environment, but not to the point where you are getting distracted and spending the whole time looking around.

So, with your eyes softly focused in front of you,

begin to walk, being aware as you lift, move and place
each foot. To help you concentrate you can silently
repeat, 'Lifting ... moving ... placing' with each step.
This movement can be very slow and ponderous, or at
a slightly faster speed to energise you, or at a normal
walking speed to loosen and release tension. The speed
will be determined by your ability to concentrate on
the movement and by what feels comfortable.
Maintaining awareness is what matters. Your body
should be relaxed, your movements natural. Keep
breathing.

Slowly you will experience the beauty of the movement, feeling yourself sinking into that movement,
experiencing the flow of your body and breath
combined. If you are in bare feet you will experience
the warmth or coolness of the ground, and whether it
is wet or dry, hard or soft, bumpy or smooth. If you are
wearing shoes you will notice the feeling of the shoe
on your foot, the sound of your shoe on the ground.
When you come to turn at the end of your path, do so
with awareness, pausing for a moment to focus on the
change in movement.

When you finish, just stand completely still for a few
moments, aware of your breath and body. Feel the
depth of stillness. Give thanks for this.

Tapes and Workshops

Details of relaxation and meditation tapes, and a list of workshops, are available from Eddie and Debbie Shapiro, c/o Piatkus Books, 5 Windmill Street, London W1P 1HF. Tapes available include:

SAMADHI – *Witness Meditation* and *Breath Awareness Meditation*. These two practices are aimed at stabilising the mind, developing clarity, self-awareness and innate wisdom. These are the foundation for all meditation practices.

METTA – *Loving Kindness Meditation* to dissolve emotional traumas and develop true compassion for both yourself and others; and *Forgiveness Meditation* to release feelings of revenge, pain, shame or guilt and allow mercy and healing to fill your heart.

KARUNA – *Loving Heart Meditation* to open to the abiding love that is your true nature; and *Heart-centred Inner Conscious Relaxation* to release unconscious emotional tension.

CHIDAKASH – *Chakra Meditation* to awaken your highest potential through the chakras or energy centres; and *Five Element Visualisation* to free areas of blocked energy and develop higher consciousness.

SAMATA-TWO – *Inner Conscious Relaxation* practices to release unconscious levels of stress, clear the mind of deep-rooted fears and tension, and discover a lasting peace and innate joy.

ANAMAYA – *Inner Healing Visualisation* to go within yourself to communicate with your body and gain guidance for healing; and *Bodymind Awareness Relaxation* to bring appreciation, healing, love and ease to each part of your body.

Bibliography

BANCROFT, Anne, *The Spiritual Journey*, Element, 1991.

BLOOM, William, *First Steps*, Findhorn Press, 1993.

CHÖDRÖN, Pema, *The Wisdom of No Escape*, Shambhala Publications, 1991.

FOX, Matthew, *Original Blessing*, Bear & Co., 1983.

GOLDSTEIN, Joseph, *Insight Meditation*, Gill & Macmillan, 1993.

GOLDSTEIN, Joseph and Kornfield, Jack, *Seeking the Heart of Wisdom*, Shambhala, 1987.

HARRISON, Eric, *Teach Yourself to Meditate*, Piatkus, 1993.

KABAT-ZINN, Jon, *Mindfulness Meditation*, Piatkus, 1994.

KORNFIELD, Jack, *A Path with Heart*, Bantam, 1993.

LEVINE, Stephen, *Guided Meditations, Explorations and Healings*, Gateway Books 1991.

LOZOFF, Bo, *We're All Doing Time*, The Human Kindness Foundation, 1985.

MCBETH, Jessica, *Moon over Water*, Gateway Books, 1990.

MCINNES, Sister Elaine and Chubb, Sandy, *Becoming Free*

Through Meditation and Yoga, The Prison Phoenix Trust, 1995.

MORROW, Lance, in *Time* magazine, 3 January 1994.

SALZBERG, Sharon, *Lovingkindness*, Shambhala Publications, 1995.

SHAPIRO, Debbie, *Your Body Speaks Your Mind*, Piatkus, 1996.

SHAPIRO, Eddie, *Inner Conscious Relaxation*, Element, 1990.

SHAPIRO, Eddie and Debbie, *A Time for Healing*, Piatkus, 1994.

SUZUKI, D.T., *Essays in Zen Buddhism*, Luzac & Co., 1927.

TAI SITU, Rinpoche, *The Way Ahead*, eds Shapiro, Eddie and Debbie, Element, 1992.

THICH NHAT HANH, *The Heart of Understanding*, Parallax Press, 1996.

TOLLIFSON, Joan, *Bare Bones Meditation: Waking Up from the Story of My Life*, Harmony Books, 1992.

TRUNGPA, Chögyam, *Shambhala*, Shambhala Publications, 1984.

WATTS, Alan, *Meditation*, Celestial Arts, 1974.

Index

Italics denote practices

Acceptance 8, 51, 52, 55–6, 57, 115
Adrenalin 19–20, 21, 24
Ahimsa 60
Anger 14, 15, 17, 22, 24, 28, 32, 34, 40, 56, 57, 61, 63, 144
Anytime Metta 58
Appreciation 46
Awareness 32

Blood pressure 14, 15, 19, 23, 24
Body scan 18
Brain waves 24
Breath 8–9, 45, 75, 77, 81, 112, 151–4
Breathing practice 75, 151–4
   Breath Awareness Meditation 154
   Breathing In, Breathing Out 147

Just Breathing 115
   Soft Breath Meditation 12
Buddha 4, 28, 43, 64
Buddhism 8, 25, 55, 95

Candle gazing 112, 162
Candle Gazing Meditation 162
Change 41–2
Clarifying Priorities 35
Clothing 73, 131
Commitment 32, 33–6, 128
Compassion 14, 51, 53, 55, 57, 59–60, 71–2
Concentration 111–2

Distraction 76, 114–5, 143
Doubt 3, 8, 31, 32, 44, 64

Ego 51, 55, 56, 95
Energy changes 121–2
Engler, Jack 51

Extending Appreciation Meditation 46

Fear 3, 8, 22, 24, 28, 31, 32, 38, 40, 42, 54, 56, 58, 64, 115, 144
Fearlessness 25, 59
Forgiveness 55, 56, 60–4, 167–8
Forgiveness Meditation 168
Fox, Matthew 6

Generosity 54, 57

Happiness 3–5, 6, 10–12, 25, 36, 37, 41, 45, 53
Healing 50, 56, 58, 83, 94, 95, 96–100
Healing Heart Meditation 65
Heart rate 19, 23–4
Harmlessness 60
Holden, Miranda 161
Holden, Robert 5

ICR – *see* Relaxation
Identities 36–40, 62
Inner Conscious Relaxation – *see* Relaxation
Insight 45
Inter-connectedness 45–6

Judgement 145
Journeying 44–5, 50, 69, 119, 120–22
Joy 4, 5, 6, 11, 25, 40, 46, 53
Just Being 29
Just Breathing Meditation 115

Kabat-Zinn, John 114

Kindness 51, 52, 53, 55–6, 558, 63
Kornfield, Jack, 50, 52

Labels 36–9, 40, 64
Levine, Stephen 40
Love 29, 55
Loving Kindness 14, 55–6, 58, 60
Loving self 55, 57
Loving others 55, 57, 58

Magic 116
Mantra 112, 159–61
Mantra Meditation 160
McBeth, Jessica 112
Meditation 3–4, 6, 8–9, 11, 12, 31, 34, 35, 40, 50, 56, 64, 111–2, 114–22, 125–6
    Effects of 24, 114–5
    How to practice 119, 120, 149–50
Meditation cushions 134, 135
Meditation stools, 135, 138
Metta 14, 55, 56, 57–9, 163–7
Metta Meditation 164
Motivation 35, 118

Noting and Labelling 39
Noting and naming 40

Opposite sensations 82

Pain 21, 53, 56, 57, 60, 61, 115, 141–3
Patience 44, 55, 63
Place 73–5, 127, 129–30
Posture 73–4, 132–40

Posture Perfect 141
Prayer 161
Prayer 161

Ramana Maharshi 49
Relaxation 6, 7, 9, 11, 21, 24,
  31, 35, 50, 51, 56, 64, 74–8,
  94
    Inner Conscious
      Relaxation 7–8, 14,
      24–5, 70, 76, 81–5
Inner Conscious Relaxation
  practices:
    Instant ICR 78
    ICR No.1 85
    ICR No.2 90
Relaxation response 23–5, 35,
  81
Resolve 83–4
Rotation of consciousness 81

Salzberg, Sharon 5, 55
Sankalpa 83–4
Satchidananda, Swami 7, 34
Satyananda, Swami 7
Self, deficient 50, 51, 52
    sufficient 51
Self-esteem 8
Self transformation 51
Sleepiness 76, 77–8, 146–7
Soft Breath Meditation 12
Stress 5, 9, 15–7, 19–22, 25,
  28–9, 34, 42, 51, 75, 76, 83,
  100

Stress-related illnesses 14–5,
  16, 17, 19–20, 21–2
Surrender 44

Tai Situ, Rinpoche 60
Tapes 174
Teachers – need for? 123–4
Thich Nhat Hanh 46, 123–4
Time 33, 34, 35, 70–3, 112,
  115, 127–9
Trungpa, Chögyam 118, 132
Trust 44

Visualisation 6, 82–3, 94–105,
  146
    for healing 96–100
    for stress release 100–2
    for self-renewal 102–4
Visualisation practices:
    Hot Hands 97
    Trading Places with the
      Buddha 102
    Journey to Inner Truth 105

Walking meditation 171
Walking Meditation 172
Watts, Alan 6, 12
Witness meditation 156
Witness Meditation 156
Workshops 174

Yoga 9, 25
Yoga nidra 7